Successful
Enjoyable
Selling

HOW TO GET THE BEST
OUT OF YOUR CAREER

Paul W. Richards, MBA

Successful *Enjoyable* Selling

HOW TO GET THE BEST OUT OF YOUR CAREER

By Paul W. Richards, MBA

Published by:

Rainier Publishing
P.O. Box 46491
Seattle, WA 98146

Copyright © 1996 by Paul W. Richards
Printed in the United States of America

ISBN 0-9649313-8-9 : $9.95

Library of Congress Catalog Card Number: 95-92731

Contents

The purpose of this book is to provide a framework of understanding that will help you discover financial success *and* personal enjoyment in the selling profession. In addition to current sales professionals, anyone thinking about undertaking sales as a career will benefit from this book. The information applies whether you sell a product or service. Most selling books do a good job teaching techniques that lead to a sale and assume that, as a salesperson, your only goal is to make money. While most individuals initially choose a sales career to make money, sooner or later they desire job fulfillment as well. Job security and financial success are as important as ever, but today most of us want more than just a healthy paycheck.

A successful enjoyable selling career requires more than an aggressive desire to win. Selling can be, and should be, fun, but it takes some knowledge and effort. The key to both financial success and personal enjoyment in selling lies in respect.

You will be successful in all meanings of the word when you have the respect of your company and your customers. The information and insights this book provides will help you gain this respect from your company and your customers, but most of all, you will respect yourself as a sales professional more than ever.

Most of us want to live productive and enjoyable lives, contributing to society and our profession, while at the same time utilizing our skills. The goal of this book is to assist you in achieving both sales success and job satisfaction. From this day forward when you read or hear the word "success," expand your own paradigm to include job satisfaction! It is possible to achieve both financial success and job satisfaction in selling and indeed the two complement each other. Find anyone that is successful financially and happy in their personal life, and you will find that they *enjoy* their work. My promise to you is that when you finish this book you will know what action you need to take to make your sales career more enjoyable. Success will certainly follow.

This book is not meant to be a comprehensive book on selling. If you are currently in sales, your company probably has or will put you through the type of training customized for your industry. Selling techniques are discussed in this book, but the main purpose is to provide you with a broad foundation for selling success. There are numerous books and tapes available packed with details on the techniques of selling. Complete books are available on the single aspect of closing the sale and you may want to read some of these later.

This book is a guidebook that will supplement your current knowledge regardless if are a beginner or a veteran sales professional. It will not only help you succeed in reaching your sales goals, but more importantly, it will help you enjoy the journey along the way. It will help you through tough spots in your selling career whether these are brought on by your own thinking, your customer, or your company.

This book is different than others in that it is your home base to come back to when you feel overwhelmed and disoriented. Think of this book as you own personal mentor. Use it as a workbook, customize it, write in it and complete all the exercises. Very little time is required and you will find the payoff invaluable.

Many times the only things you can change about your work situation lie inside your own mind. You cannot change your customer's personalities or your company strategy; you *can* change the way you react to the problems they cause. Your customers and your company will cause problems, and dealing with them is a continuous challenge. Whining never helps, but closing your eyes to the truth will not lead to true selling success and job fulfillment.

Whether it is work or play, you must learn that satisfaction in life comes from striving toward goals that you deem worthy and enjoying the process along the way. Often we find that reaching a goal is not as exciting as the process itself. Developing the ability to keep focused on the larger purpose of your goals helps us weather problems that inevitably occur.

The key to selling success lies in helping customers find solutions to problems by uncovering their needs and wants. Once this is understood, we can all learn to slow down, listen, and invest time with people. A customer is an individual person. If you truly care about them you can become a consultant that helps them find solutions to problems rather than just another salesperson trying to push something on them.

Profits and production goals are a company's number one priority, but it is the duty of the salesperson to keep the *customer's* needs first. If your product or service does not offer the best solution to your customers needs, you should move on to others that you can help. You may discover you need to sell a different product!

In this day and age of high tech, rapid change, opportunities are numerous for lucrative and enjoyable selling careers. A truly caring, honest, sincere, and competent sales professional can write his or her own ticket to financial success and personal fulfillment. Promise yourself that you will strive to be this type of professional.

This first section of this book deals with an important ingredient to complete success in selling—understanding your company and its business. How does your company's marketing strategy affect your day-to-day selling efforts? The problems and solutions to company situations, the importance of "knowing your stuff," and differences in selling styles between industries and companies are all analyzed thoroughly.

The second section deals with elements of success for self-improvement. Attitude, planning and goal setting, personal time, and meditation, are just part of this important section.

Finally, the last section of the book reviews key elements of selling success—understanding personality styles, purpose statements, effective questions, and closing the sale. Again, all of this information can supplement any of the current philosophies or techniques you may currently be using.

Remember, win-win situations can occur in sales; the customer does not have to "lose" for you to win. In today's global and competitive business environment, the customer must win in order for you to earn their loyalty.

The way you think affects everything you do and the way you respond to others. Promise yourself that you will think positively about your career every minute of every day. Selling is a noble profession today more than ever! Global competition has made it necessary for companies to spend more on selling efforts. Gone are the days when you could build a better mousetrap and customers would line up outside your door.

Positive thought carries over into every part of our lives and it has the power to make good things happen. Positive thoughts are the foundation for a successful enjoyable sales career.

This book addresses the major issues that determine the outcome of your success as a salesperson. It provides the information you need to build a successful selling career. In our society success is usually measured in financial and quantitative terms. Sell more, earn more, have more. While this is important to nearly everyone, you probably desire the qualitative aspects of job satisfaction in addition to the quantitative financial rewards from your work. Success in financial terms can be gained without understanding the principles in this book, but enjoyment will be fleeting.

Many people have stepped on others to "succeed" with the idea that when they reach a certain station in life they will be fulfilled. Many times these people learn that they should have enjoyed the journey along the way. This book will help you plan your selling career so that you get the best out of it. Good luck in your profession!

Part One

Foundations for Understanding Your Business

Chapter One

How to think like a Marketing Manager

To truly understand your organization and work effectively and happily within it, you must understand your company's marketing strategy. Once this is accomplished you will know what to expect in terms of management directives, product developments, and employment issues. We will look at marketing theory and strategy, and then how this relates to different company strategies and missions.

Consider the type of industry your company represents. Industries tend to use varying strategies based on the customer they serve. An automobile manufacturer will market its product differently than would a consumer product manufacturer. Also software and high technology companies will change strategies much faster than insurance companies. The point is to know what to realistically expect from your organization.

Consider the customer your company serves and the competition that challenges your company's product or service. This knowledge can help you understand what to expect with regard to policies and directives from management. Is this the type of organization you should be a part of? (In chapter six we will look at how your values should match your company's but keep this question in mind.)

Many good salespeople have given up on sales because they

felt they were not "cut out for it." While this may be true in some cases, many times it the simple problem of a poor match between company, industry, and salesperson.

One of the common myths is that good salespeople are born with the gift to sell. Good salespeople are made not born. All good salespeople are constant students of their company, profession, and industry. A good understanding of the selling profession requires a knowledge of marketing.

Once you consider your organization's industry and customer base as a foundation of understanding how you fit in, you can look at the specific strategy. You can learn much about what your organization stands for by simply reading and interpreting your company's mission statement. Someone in human resources or at the home office should have access to this statement. (If your company does not have one, you still have valuable information: they may not know which direction they are headed.) The mission statement should reveal something about the company's customers, and products, and/or services.

Throughout this chapter and this book, the word product and service can be interchanged. Service-based businesses have grow significantly and will continue to be an integral part of our economy. Many economists believe service-based companies will contribute more to our economy than manufacturing-based companies in the future. Do not confuse the word service as it applies to service-based industries with service in the customer-service context. Service-based businesses include but are not limited to: Financial, computer, accounting, legal, janitorial, transportation, and communication. Good customer service is used to enhance a company's market offering whether it is a product or a service that is being sold. It is not uncommon for a service based company, such as an airline to promote their customer-service as their strong point.

The "Four-P's" of marketing

How do companies implement their strategies? The Four P's of the marketing mix refers to the tools available to marketers— Product, Price, Promotion, and Place. The amount of each element used is referred to as the Marketing Mix. Each element plays a distinct part in the marketing process.

A **product**'s packaging design, brand name, features and quality, are all part of this element of the four P's. Services are also packaged but rely more on promotion and the quality of the presentation to create the desired image. When purchasing a service the customer does not get a tangible item, but does benefit in a functional or emotional way from the service. A good example is the airline industry. One airline may position themselves as the most "on time" airline, while another may emphasize the warm feeling you get from the friendly service. Both companies are selling the same service but are *positioning* their offer differently. More on positioning shortly. Improving any or all of these aspects of "Product" can increase sales on an otherwise slow moving product or service.

The **price** element consists of discounts, allowances and payment terms. Setting a price may seem simple, but many aspects must be considered when determining the correct price for a product or service—competition, market trends, industry breakthroughs, and general demand. Payment terms can make a tremendous difference in a company's profit from quarter-to-quarter.

Promotion includes coupons, advertising, public relations, direct marketing, and the salesforce—any vehicle to get the word out to the customer. TV, radio, newspapers, magazines, and billboards are just a few of the media used to advertise a product or service. Coupons and special offers are printed in conventional publications and formats, but also on the back of sales receipts. Companies are teaming up to bundle their products with those of other companies; the result is a powerful synergy. Take out pizza companies offer free soft drinks with a minimum order. This benefits both the pizza company and the soft drink company. For the soft drink company, giving out free product is more cost effective than spending cash on promotion. By offering the free soft drinks, the pizza company has enhanced their market offer without slashing prices or skimping on the quality of their product. The sky is the limit in this category of the marketing mix, and creativity can be critical to a company's overall success.

Finally **place** of distribution includes channels, locations, inventory, etc. Depending on the industry and the customer the company serves, distribution channels can vary widely. Direct sales and retail sales via distribution warehouses are two of the most common distribution channels. There is plenty of room for creativity as companies have discovered 800 numbers, direct mail selling, and even home shopping by television. How a company allocates its budget to the different parts of the marketing mix depends on where they stand competitively and where they wish to develop business in the future. Some of this is determined, to a great degree, by the company's over-all strategy.

The "cash cow"

Every company has a product or service that is the "cash cow"—the real profit center for the business. Profits from this slower-growing product or service may or may not be skimmed off to develop new products or "stars." This concept is called the Boston Consulting Group matrix, named for the same. Any marketing text will explain this in greater detail, but for our purposes know that your organization has a cash cow product or service. The goal of progressive companies is to invest today in tomorrow's cash cows.

Ford's cash cow today may well be its Taurus sedan, but it will not be forever. You can be sure that Ford engineers are hard at work designing its future replacement. Microsoft Corporation relies on its DOS and Windows operating system software to fund new ventures. These new ventures are referred to as Stars, if they do well, and Dogs if they do not. One recent Dog of Microsoft's was the financial program Money. This program never made a dent in the market share of the leading personal financial program Quicken. It is typical for companies to have several Dogs before discovering the Star product or service of the future.

The way in which your company invests its profits is directly related to management's philosophy. In some privately-held companies the owners have no intention of growing a business, and have the goal of enriching their life today at the company's expense. They may take all the profits from their cash cow and spend them on executive perks or add them to their personal estate. Most companies invest these profits for future growth and to enhance shareholder value and profitability.

All products and services have a life cycle

In a typical situation, a product life cycle will progress from introduction to growth to maturity, and finally, will decline over time. Usually a company will fight hard to keep a product in the growth phase and prefer maturity, with flat sales, to that of a decline. The reason for this is simple; it is expensive to market a new product and success is far from guaranteed.

Maintaining a profitable product or service is desirable. During the introduction phase, a company will use a varying combination of high or low price and promotion to achieve different goals. A product launched with a high promotion level and a low price is implemented to penetrate the market rapidly. The goal is to grab as much market share as possible in the shortest amount of time. If a market is large, highly aware of the product, but very price sensitive, a low promotion-low price or *slow penetration strategy* is best. This is just one example of how different combinations of the marketing mix can be used to achieve different results. Everything costs money, and with a finite amount of funds to market a product, managers want the most efficient combination of the four p's.

During the growth phase of a product's life cycle, a company will add product features, distribution channels, new line additions, and lower prices at times to attract new customers. Momentum has built during this phase and enhancing all the elements of the marketing mix maximizes sales.

The mature phase of a product's life cycle is more challenging in some ways—sales have leveled off and more money needs to be spent on promotion in order to achieve the same level of sales. Products that decline can be brought back to life and grow again, but it is rare. It is difficult to develop a successful product or service—large amounts of time and money are invested. All efforts are expended to prevent the product's decline since it is more cost effective to spend money *before* a decline.

The Volume Leaders (companies with high market share) are usually segmented by Quality, Service, and Price. They specialize in one of these three areas. There are some niche players that find a special area of consumer need that the big guys cannot fill. This is the definition of **niche**—a small market segment that is not currently being served by any company. A good example is the toothpaste market. The big companies such as Proctor and Gamble often consider a market with a potential of a few million dollars as too small to deal with. However, to a small company, a few million in sales is a business!

Tom's of Maine toothpaste has carved out a niche in the toothpaste market with a product consisting of all natural ingredients. If this market grows to a greater level you can be sure that Proctor and Gamble will enter this market as well. This is exactly what happened with baking soda toothpaste. It was not until Arm and Hammer chipped away a significant portion of market share that Proctor and Gamble and other large companies responded with their own baking soda products. The process continues as new products gain market share and the older products die off because of their presence.

These rapid dynamic changes in the business environment often lead larger companies to buy smaller niche players. Small software companies, often with only one product on the market, are being bought by larger corporations at a feverish rate. The microbrew market is an example of one that has threatened the big boys. Redhook Brewery in the Seattle area has made such an impact on the beer market that Anheuser Busch recently agreed to buy part of that business. Pepsi has approached Starbucks Coffee Company to form an alliance in order to develop a coffee beverage. With competition from companies such as Snapple Beverage, the last thing Pepsi needs is to miss out on a growth market such as specialty coffees.

The real estate, financial, and insurance industries have also had tumultuous changes in recent years. Acquisitions of smaller companies have led to megacompanies in these and other service industries. Technology has changed the way these industries do business and this trend will increase in the near future as alliances are formed between television networks, telephone, and computer companies. Advances in digital technology and computer software have made it possible.

Technology and information-service-based industries change more rapidly than manufactured goods industries. Replacements for toothpaste, soap, oil and textiles, are difficult to find. Technology such as voice-mail can replace electronic mail or vice-versa.

It may be difficult to determine where your company fits, in relation to the competition. Microsoft is the clear market leader when it comes to PC operating system software. But in other segments, such as financial application programs, Microsoft is a challenger. Whether your company is a service-based business or manufacturer of hard goods, you will find that there are as many different classifications as there are distinct business segments.

Is your company a leader or a follower?

Being a follower is not all that bad. It is difficult to invent and market new products that yield a profit—most have an extremely high failure rate. 3M is one of the few companies that is truly innovative. They invent new uses for existing technologies and even invent new technology based on market demand. A new chemical compound produced by one division can be used to manufacture a new product by another unrelated division. A lucrative market opportunity will encourage investment to produce a new product to serve that market. In either case, numerous other companies will follow their lead and spin off products to supply the market demand 3M creates.

Many products are easy to copy, and services are even easier to copy. Patents and copyrights cover material that is very specific in nature and not ideas or concepts. Even drug companies that invent a new chemical compound can hold a patent for only several years. After that time others can come out with their own product based on the compound.

Often it is a better business decision to wait and see how one company does in a market before entering it. It has been said that it is better to have the second bite of a good apple, than the first bite of a bad one.

So where is your company? Are they a market leader, market challenger, market follower, or a market niche player? Sometimes it is not so easy to tell. Generally there are some indications that point to one area. Many companies operate as the market leader in one product, a follower or challenger in another, and yet a niche player in another. These roles may be reversed in different regions of the country or the world.

Low-Cost Leader or Differentiator

Companies usually operate as a *low-cost leader*, or a *product differentiator*. The differentiator's selling position is: "You cannot compare our product to product X; our product is so different it would be like comparing apples to oranges." Pointing out features that demonstrate this difference is a key strategy in promotion and packaging. The low cost operator says, "our product is the same as product X, but costs less."

"Private-label" or store-brand consumer products such as mouthwash, soaps, cereals, and other basic food items are good examples of a low-cost market position. Many large grocery store chains have developed their own spin-offs of the big brands. These have taken away significant market share from the big popular brands of Proctor and Gamble and other large companies. Many of these larger companies have lowered prices on many popular brands and have even entered the business of making "generics" as they are sometimes referred to. They may own the manufacturing facility where the various grocery chains manufacture these low cost copy-cat products. While they lose some business to competition on the store shelf, they gain business at the manufacturing end.

Fill in some answers to the following questions and elaborate with extra ideas and insights you may have regarding your current company. Even if you are a veteran salesperson you may want to ask these questions to some managers at the middle to upper level to make sure you get a clear picture of your organization. Two heads are always better than one, even the brightest people gain better perspective through a consensus.

1. What words describe the industry your company is in? Service based, or manufacturer?_____fast changing, high technology, cyclical (autos etc.), non-cyclical (soap, etc.), slow growing, fast growing?_____

_____

_____

2. Describe the typical customer profile. Do they reorder regularly? One-time-only sale?_____

_____

3. Describe your competition. What direct competition do you have?_____

_____

What indirect competition to you have? (i.e. VCR's and movie theaters compete even though they are different types of businesses. Banks, and insurance companies compete with stockbrokers for investment dollars, even though they are all in different businesses.)

_____

4. How are your products priced and positioned in the market-place versus your competition?_____

5. What other variables explain your company's philosophies and values (review your companys mission statement?)

_____

_____

_____

The above answers may reveal some interesting aspects that you were previously unaware of. You may discover that your organization is poised for excellent growth prospects in the future. Conversely, you may discover that it is time to look for a position with a different company or in a different industry. At the very least you will gain a better understanding than you previously had regarding your company's policies and strategies.

Target Marketing

Out of the entire universe of possible buyers, companies must determine which *segments* of the market will yield the best sales. In the past it was possible to advertise to everyone but today it makes sense to be more selective. Based on market research companies will *target* certain segments of a particular market. Markets can be segmented based on any number of characteristics—age, race, sex, religion, lifestyle and socioeconomic class.

A company may select middle-class 40 to 50-year-old men as the segment of the market to target for its golfing product. The product, promotion, price, and place of distribution are all customized to market the product to this group of consumers. Later the company may decide that 20 to 30-year-old women should be targeted as well. Changing the color and size of the product, adapting advertising and promotion, are all it takes sometimes to tap into other markets. The potential to increase sales through different mixes of the 4 P's is limited only by the imagination.

Positioning and Brand Recognition

Positioning refers to the image a product has in the minds of the target customers. Some products are positioned naturally, based on their inherent characteristics, and others are turned into something different through advertising.

Positioning is based on human emotions and traits that influence the buying decision—desire for status, fear of loss, need for security and acceptance. These are all motives used to create advertising.

Insurance and financial product companies capitalize on the fear of loss and the need for security. An illustration showing a young family that is dependent on a provider creates a compelling reason to buy life insurance. A commercial depicting a financially-strapped elderly couple plays on a fear of poverty and encourages investing.

Car companies can utilize, fear, security, or status as motives to buy their products. Volvo emphasizes its brand's safety over all other features and uses a baby in some of its ads. The caption mentions "wrapping your child in a 3,000 pound security blanket."

Porshe has positioned its product to consumers that desire affluence, status, and youthful thrills. In an effort to expand sales from its traditional target market of married couples with children, Volvo has tried to target a younger market segment. The creation of a sportier Volvo, complete with youthful TV advertising, shows its commitment to a market expansion.

The position a product holds in a person's mind in very difficult to change. Once accepted in one position it is likely to stay there. This happens over time but basically boils down to *brand recognition*. To most people the word Volvo creates an image of a safe reliable family car, while Porshe conjures up images of a youthful stylish sportscar. These positions or perceptions of these products were created over many years. Changing the position in the mind of the consumer is possible, but very unlikely, and not without spending a lot of money over an extended period of time.

People expect to find lower quality items at K-Mart but not at Bloomingdales or Saks Fifth Avenue. K-Mart has worked hard to overcome the "cheap" position in the minds of consumers. It has been utilizing actress-model Jacqueline Smith to create an image of a store that has *value*—good items at good prices. McDonald's has tried very hard to win over the dinner crowd at its restaurants with little luck. To most consumers, McDonalds will always mean an inexpensive predictable quality lunch or breakfast. The 7-11 stores are known for their convenient locations and hours of operation, not their prices or selection.

Marketers must be careful how they initially position a product or service. Spending the resources to create the best, most profitable position is better than wasting money later trying to undo what is already done.

As a salesperson, consider your company's position in the customer's's mind. Selling techniques can go a long way to overcome customer objections and buying resistance, but to try changing a well-established perception is difficult, if not impossible. How can you expect to overcome a customer's perception in one or even twenty sales calls when the perception was created through years of advertising?

If you sell a premium product or service that is widely recognized, capitalize on it. "That machine is the real *cadillac* of machines," is one example of a strong brand image. Some people are used to referring to items by brand names—"hand me a *Kleenex*," or "wipe that up with a *Scottowel*," are just two examples that demonstrate the power of positioning and brand recognition. Get all the mileage you can out of a good reputation because your company has paid for this admiration.

On the other hand, if your product has the reputation of the low cost version, capitalize on that. Never try to make it something it obviously is not.

Building Brand Equity

Positioning in the customer's mind, if done consistently and aggressively, builds a *brand equity*. The Coca-Cola company has a value based on its physical and financial assets—real estate, equipment, inventory, bonds, investments and cash. But almost more important is the earning potential the Coke brand has now and in the future. A dollar value can be placed on this, and it is the company's best asset since it determines present and future sales.

Brand recognition is the first step in creating a sale. Customer's have to know about a product before they can consider it in their realm of purchasing choices. Say the word "Coke" to people anywhere in the world, and the majority will know what it is. This took a lot of money over several decades of advertising. Determining the value of a brand, or its brand equity, is in large part determined by this long-term investment in addition to potential sales.

The Nutrasweet brand of sweetener has wide recognition because of a creative idea. The parent company of this brand had the foresight to negotiate with major soft drink companies to grant them the permission to print the word and logo "Nutrasweet" on all soft drinks that contained this ingredient. People have long forgotten other artificial sweeteners because Nutrasweet has won that position in their minds.

Intel, the microprocessor company, did a similar thing when it convinced computer manufacturers to place the "Intel inside" logo on the outside of all personal computers.

Both of these companies know the value of a widely-recognized brand name. Although both brands are hidden inside the final product, these companies refused to let their names be hidden from the consumer. Because of this, they have the ability to springboard off this recognition should they decide to launch other products.

Fragmented Markets

This important concept explains a lot of the change that occurs within companies or industries. Markets usually start out serving a small amount of needs for a relatively small group of customers. The soft drink market provides a good example.

Years ago Coke and Pepsi dominated markets offering colas to nearly everyone. The soft drink market has gradually fragmented into smaller markets—seltzer water, ice teas, and flavored drinks such as Snapple. Coke has responded with its own fruit-flavored drinks to combat this challenge to its flagship product. In the past the entire soft drink market was composed of consumers of all types; today it is more varied and specialized. While the younger crowd is the primary market for soft drinks, baby boomers have their own unique demands. Boomers command attention from companies because of the size of this group.

Wants are different than needs. We all *need* very little but want quite a bit. Often we convince ourselves that these wants are genuine needs. Twenty years ago the answering machine was not necessary; today we feel lost without one. We could live without it; if something is important the person will call back. Often we do not know what we want until it is available.

The toothpaste market provides an example of how markets get complex and fragmented with dozens of varieties, and then revert back to a less fragmented state. In the 1960's, cavity-preventing toothpaste was *the* new product for dental care. There were toothpowders available previously, but the new products were clinically proven to prevent tooth decay. Then came the toothpastes that promised fresher breath. Others promised whiter teeth. Much of this relates directly to the above explanation of positioning. But since that time, many varieties have evolved—baking soda, gel, tartar control, and recently baking soda with peroxide. The market is very crowded with multiple varieties, but is beginning to evolve further as old varieties die out. Promising cavity prevention is no longer enough.

Usually markets will go through a "shakeout" with some of the varieties fading away, leaving the stronger brands to take up the slack. The toothpaste market is going through this now with many of the older varieties being replaced by baking soda, tartar control and whitening products.

This chapter has laid the foundation for understanding marketing strategy. Understanding marketing strategy is important because it is the starting point for the resulting sales strategy. Keep these concepts and principles in mind any time you are interpreting company policy or directives. Next we look at company situations and how you fit in to your organization.

Chapter Two

Company Situations

You represent your company, but you are employed by your customers

The healthiest attitude for any sales professional is that of a self-employed person. This does not mean that you play by your own rules and entirely ignore company directives. But it does give perspective and keep you focused on what is important and help you avoid picking battles that are futile and a waste of your time and energy. As in most things in life, balance is the key. When you understand your company's overall strategy, selling strategy, and your own attitudes, you will naturally make the best decision when you eventually get stuck between a customer's request and the company's policy.

We will look at the importance of attitude in the second section of this book, but for now consider your interaction with your customers and your company.

Most sales professionals think of themselves as working for their company. After all, that is where the paycheck, and bonus, and commission checks come from. Ultimately, however, you work for your customers. If you put their needs first, you will sell more and enjoy the process along the way as well.

Secondly, you work for yourself. Think of yourself as a business asset that you must continually work to improve. You can increase the value of this asset through industry training and sales learning. When you put this paradigm in place you will automatically be of more value to your customers, yourself, and your company. You will also be of more value to any other company, and this is the ultimate in job security. What a confidence booster!

When you incorporate this type of thinking you will easily weather the conflicts that inevitably occur between you and your customers, and between you and your company. The business environment is very dynamic today and these elements are constantly changing. You are changing, and chances are do not have exactly the same needs and desires you did two or three or more years ago. Companies are changing faster than ever before in history. Think in terms of what your customers need and you will be able to clearly see if your company is on track with the same philosophy. A company's current management may neglect the true needs of the customer.

Know how your product or service benefits your customer

What does the customer gain from your product or service? What do they need now that they did not need just a short while ago? You must answer these questions *now* before you can ever begin to really become a resource to your customer.

List ten benefits that your customers or prospects can gain from your product or service. List the ten best but do not stop there if you can think of more.

Also make some notes on how your customers and their

business may have changed. This will give you insights as to how your product or service can be utilized in new ways perhaps not thought of. If you have not been in your business very long, talk to the superstars in your company and/or industry. You may want to talk to customers that are happy with your product or service. Consider your company's ideas of what your customers need, but do not be limited by these ideas.

1._____
2._____
3._____
4._____
5._____
6._____
7._____
8._____
9._____
10._____

Refer to this list often as you plan your goals and selling strategy. You may even want to write it in your daily planner or on a 3 X 5 card and put where you see it every day. The advantage of knowing how your customer benefits from your product is twofold. Obviously knowing how the customer benefits from your product helps sell it. But equally important is that, once you know the key elements of what your product does for the customer, you will recognize policies or strategies that may threaten or weaken your competitive advantage.

Put your customer's needs first

It is not an easy task to put your customer's concerns first. After all you need to make money. If you are a straight commission sales person the challenge is even greater. The temptation to sell something, anything, every day is great. After all you are a sales person and you and your company have goals based on quotas. The numbers are tracked monthly if not daily. Sales representatives of pharmaceutical and consumer products companies usually manage many different products. These large companies have added new products in recent years in order to make up for flat sales of mature products. The desired growth rate was not attainable with the "old products" so new products were added to grow the bottom line. This is a logical solution to the problem of flat sales.

In most cases sales management decides that calling on customers more frequently is optimal, since studies reveal that prospects do not buy until after the fifth or sixth sales attempt. Without evaluating the study that determined this, suffice it to say that these formulas do not work for all customers. Management's conclusion: Make a larger number of calls to the same customers over the course of a year. More calls, more sales—simple!

Ah, but it is not that simple. People are complicated with unique individual needs. When we treat them all the same we are not becoming the resource that we desire to become. We are not treating them the way they deserve to be treated—as individuals with their own special needs.

Each customer is unique

Some customers do not want to be visited frequently. They do not want to feel like just another stop along your route. Showing up to call on a customer because some study says it is best, can be harmful to your credibility. When you show up frequently without a real strong purpose for doing so, you appear to be a person that is not very busy without much to offer. Their reply when they see you should not be, "Oh, it's you again. Weren't you just here?" We will talk more about the importance of purpose statements in chapter ten.

Some customers may require more frequent attention. Due to special circumstances you may need to stop by every week or even every few days to satisfy a customer. Consider each customer's individual needs before deciding how often to call on them.

Management always feels that their programs and philosophies will help the bottom line, but, as the customer's resource and consultant, *you* should interpret the value of these programs. You must be selective about what to implement, based on the ultimate concern for creating *value* for your customer. Customize the program to your customer's unique and specific needs.

Have Empathy for your management—but do what is best for your customers

Managers today are in a tough position. Have empathy for your upper sales and marketing management. They must be budget-based according to predicted sales, and hence become focused on achieving these numbers. Shareholders demand profits or new managers. It is impossible not to become extremely numbers-oriented in this environment. If your common sense and knowledge tell you that a program, product, or sales strategy will not be best for your customer, alter it so that it is. It is usually possible to alter programs and make them work to offer the customer a benefit. But if the program goes against what you know is in the best interest of your customer it probably is. Do not do it!

The worst that will happen is you will discover you should be working for the competition, another company, or, in another industry.

Obviously you want to communicate to sales management about ways to improve the program. You owe it to yourself and your company to try your best to implement a program or strategy. Very often if the strategy or product or service is a poor fit for the customer, it will be terminated by management in time anyway. Trust your intuition and you may save yourself frustration and, at the same time, prevent losing credibility among your customers.

Be patient and tactful when you recognize a poor strategy

This happens time and time again with companies large and small. If the majority of a company's sales force immediately recognizes a poor strategy, chances are good the program will fail for its own reasons. Many sales people today are not aware of strategic blunders since they change companies every few years. This is not enough time to learn what is important to the customer and how the company can best fulfill the customers needs. It is not uncommon for companies to change upper level managers every few years. The result of this turmoil is constant change in sales and marketing strategies. All this internal change and the customers usually change very little. The industry may change quite a bit as well, but the customer can change in smaller ways. You must know that if the product, strategy or philosophy does not serve the customers interests or needs, it will not last. Being a leader and an innovator is both respected and required in today's selling environment. While the company will fight you if you openly argue against poorly-thought-out strategies, you will be rewarded in the long run for keeping your customer's interests first.

One final note: be tactful when criticizing any program or strategy. The person you are talking to may be the one who spearheaded it. As with any business situation, diplomacy is a must. No matter how bad something seems, there is always a positive point somewhere. Always start out with positive things to say, then lead into "possible improvements." Involve the person in a conversational way so as not to sound pompous. This is especially true when talking to superiors. They expect you to act somewhat subordinate. Appease them and let them suggest some possible improvements as well. Changes are more likely to be made if *they* come up with a good idea too. This is all part of playing politics in the hierarchy of an organization. This does not mean you have to become a "yes" person. Remain aware of the power plays for status that are going on around you. Knowing how and when to suggest things is critical if you want to be heard and respected among your colleagues.

Perception is Reality

This sounds overly simplistic but is true if you think about it. How else can two people have entirely different ideas about the same situation. To someone else, their perception of the situation is reality. Keep this in mind when dealing with managers, colleagues, customers, and even friends and family. We will talk more about empathy and listening skills, but understanding individual behavior begins with accepting that things appear differently to each individual. Asking a person's opinion on something is flattering. It shows you value their ideas and, more importantly, permits them to open up to you. When you genuinely listen to a person, they often will tell you their perception of a situation and reveal why they act the way they do.

Profits vs. Sales

Sales are necessary for any organization that hopes to make a profit. But there are other aspects that determine whether or not a sale is profitable. While sales are necessary to create revenue, a company's success, and your success, is in large part determined by the profitability of each sale.

Revenue is determined by the dollar amount of sales generated over a given period of time. The Cost-of-goods-sold (COGS) minus the revenue or sales, equals the profit the company often refers to as the "bottom-line." COGS includes more than the material cost—administrative, warehousing, sales expenses, and anything else that takes away from the potential profit of a sale. Some products cost more than others to manufacture, warehouse and sell.

There are only three things a company can do to generate more profit:

- Increase the amount of sales
- Raise prices
- Decrease COGS and all other expenses

Some companies do all three at once, but usually increasing sales is the first choice. Raising prices must be done carefully after considering the customer needs and the competition's strategy. Raising prices at the wrong time can work to *decrease* sales and lose market share. Decreasing COGS and other expenses is beneficial, but not if it compromises the quality of the product. Cutting back on customer service is a great way to send customers to your competitors.

Increasing sales is the easiest and least risky option of the three. New selling techniques are sometimes all it takes quarter-to-quarter, but increasing sales long-term is not an easy undertaking. Increasing sales volume does great things for profits as well. Usually there is a certain point where sales volume changes the profitability of the sale dramatically. *Economies of scale* is one term used to refer to this break-even point. This level of sales is different for every company and every product. There is a certain level of sales that just covers expenses. For example, a company may have to produce and sell 1,000 units per day just to pay the bills. At a level of 2,000 units per day, they may earn 5% profit per unit. At a level of 2,500 units, the level may jump to 10%. But at 3,000 units it may go up to 25%. You can understand the incentive to sell 3,000 units per day. Companies often set sales quotas based more on desired profit than the actual sales potential.

There are four fundamental ways to increase sales:

- Find new uses for existing products
- Increase current usage of existing products
- Find new customers for existing products
- Market new products

The first two—finding new uses and increasing current product usage—are usually the most cost-effective ways to increase sales. Marketing managers refer to this as *market penetration*.

Getting more sales out of existing customers is the first, and least expensive, way to increase sales. Salespeople can often be creative and find a new use for a product that the marketing department had not thought of yet. Drug companies frequently work on expanding the usage of current medications. Tagamet, the popular ulcer drug, is now sold over-the-counter as a treatment for stomach upset as well. Tums has advertised that its product contains calcium; implying that the product not only works for stomach upset, but for osteoporosis as well.

Proper understanding of the product on the customer's part can sometimes increase its current usage. Perhaps the salesperson did not explain the product uses clearly enough, or maybe the customer needed to hear it several times before it really sank in. It is important to convey all the proper uses of your product or service to the customer. One good way to do this is to ask them how they are using it, rather than tell them how they should use it. Lecturing will frequently lead to head-nodding on the part of the customer without hearing what you are saying. "How are you using product X?" is a good question to ask. If they leave out a key use for your product, offer good reasons for them to try your suggestions. "Those are good uses for product X. Many of our customers have found that it works well for... as well. Will you try it this way too?" Complementing, suggesting, and then asking for a commitment to try it can go a long way to increase sales.

Finding new customers to use existing products depends on prospecting and advertising. This is sometimes referred to as a *market expansion*. You must constantly be on the lookout for new customers in your territory. As a salesperson, your key role is tracking down new customers for your product or service. The marketing department is in charge of finding new customers through advertising and promotion. But do not be afraid to suggest ideas to them. In your prospecting activities, you may discover an effective promotion or advertising idea. Suggesting it and getting it implemented will help your sales and the company's profitability as well.

Marketing new products is usually the last choice as a method of increasing sales. Often companies do this in addition to the above strategies. It is expensive and risky to develop new products that are profitable. More often than not they fail.

You are an asset *and* an expense

You are a valuable asset to your company, but are an expense to be optimized. Companies want to get the best return on their investment in their salespeople. They strive to maximize production from equipment and they expect the same from employees. This may sound a little cold, but on paper that's the way it is.

Selling costs are on the expense side of the equation and managers constantly strive to decrease expenses. Without salespeople nothing can be sold, but rest assured, your sales management must justify selling expenses on a regular basis to upper management.

Often you can justify an expense by showing how it helps increase sales and profits. The telephone is an inexpensive supplement to a personal sales call. When used together with personal calls the telephone increases customer contact and the potential for future sales. Timely phone followup can also prevent customer returns and therefore help increase bottom-line profits.

Chapter Three

Knowing Your Stuff

There are five aspects to knowing your stuff. You must know your:

1) company's products
2) competitor's products
3) industry trends and developments
4) selling and management trends and philosophies
5) customer's business needs

You must master these five aspects in order to become a true resource or "consultant" to your customer. This resource status will provide you with the financial success and personal satisfaction you seek as a sales professional. In addition to becoming a resource, you will develop valuable skills that will follow you to other jobs in the future.

Know your products

Before you can understand your customer's business you must first know your products as a foundation. A comprehensive and complete knowledge of your products or services is necessary if you are going to be thorough in finding solutions to your customer's needs. Your company will usually assist you here, but not always. Learn to ask questions anytime you feel the need to. Upon asking technical product questions, you may get a reply from managers like, "you don't need to know that to sell this!" Remember your goal is to become a true resource to your customers. You need answers to these questions in order to add to your base of product knowledge. One of the best compliments you can receive from a customer is to be asked your opinion of a product you do not sell. It communicates trust, respect, and demonstrates your value as a sales representative. It takes quite a few years to get to this point, but it is worth the invested time and effort. It almost makes the thousands of rejections received over the years worth it!

Take advantage of all company-provided training. If you feel your company does not provide enough training to meet your needs, ask for more. You may be surprised how willing your company is to provide you with funds to attend classes and seminars. If your company is small, they may have an underdeveloped training agenda simply because no one has had the time to implement one yet.

Some possible suggestions include volunteering to put together a seminar with veteran reps training newer recruits. You may want to attend some selling seminars that are offered in your area from time to time. Purchasing books and audio and video tapes and sharing them with a group in a presentation or a sales meeting is another inexpensive training idea.

Suggest ideas and you will get valuable training *and* become known as an idea person in the process. This will earn you respect from management and add to your value as a sales person. As a result you will become a valuable asset to your organization.

Volunteer to attend trade shows or conventions as these are excellent arenas to learn how your products or services fit your customer's needs, and your competitor's strategies as well. At trade shows and company meetings, become a sponge for knowledge. Ask questions to veteran reps and *listen*. People love to pass on their words of wisdom. Make sure to solicit the advice of the most successful (and happy) representatives, staying away from the old pessimistic war dogs.

Make a special effort at trade shows and conventions to talk to other company representatives. Your direct competitors may not be very open to talking with you, but others will. You add to your knowledge base when you know your industry inside and out. This adds to your credibility as a sales representative and gives you a better understanding of your customers needs—starting you on your way to consultant/resource status.

By participating in company meetings and industry trade shows you can accomplish most of what is needed of the five aspects of "knowing your stuff." But do not stop there. Listen to all the tapes and read all the books about selling you can get your hands on. You should own every sales book or tape series that has ideas you can benefit from. A year or two down the road you will need to review the concepts and ideas. Frequently trade shows can help provide insight to business trends in your industry. I cannot say enough about the importance of trade and industry shows since you get so much for such a small amount of time invested.

Know your competitors products

The second aspect, knowing your competitors products, takes just as much effort as knowing your own. As with all learning this requires a lifelong commitment. When making small talk with your customers always remember to ask "what's new out there in the marketplace?" People love to impart knowledge and help others if given the chance. You will be surprised how much they will tell you if you give them the opportunity. "You should see the new gizmo XYZ just came out with." Ask and listen and you will learn.

Reading industry journals is a must in technical sales positions, but *any* sales person can benefit from reading publications and periodicals that relate to their industry. How good a stockbroker will you be if you don't read the *Wall Street Journal every* day? How can you convince someone that you can make them more money than they could on their own if you are not as up-to-speed on financial events as they are? If you sell computer software you had better understand computer hardware, and vice versa.

Know industry trends and developments

Reading industry journals and periodicals takes care of the third aspect—industry trends and developments. But it does something more. It makes you a more interesting and well-rounded person.

Given the choice between two different sales people a customer will always spend more time talking to the more interesting one. Chit-chat about hobbies and sports more with some customers than others. Still, to be respected for knowledge regarding products and services leads to a sale more often.

Know selling trends

The fourth aspect of knowing your stuff is management trends and philosophies regarding selling. Peruse bookstores to stay in touch with what the latest business gurus have to say about your future. While these philosophies are sometimes revealed as simple buzzwords for a few years, it's important to know what management is trying to achieve. Empowerment and TQM (total quality management) are just a few of the terms that have been overused in the recent past. Many companies kid themselves into thinking they are incorporating these just to look like they are "on the cutting edge."

Ask any company if they are "customer driven" and they will all respond with a resounding Yes. Some may even show you where it is written in their mission statements. Yet, actions speak louder than words. Just because someone says they do something doesn't mean they do.

Know your customers needs

When you combine the knowledge you acquire from your sales calls, conventions or industry shows, and reading industry journals, you cover the fifth aspect of knowing your stuff. You simply ask your customers what they need. Sometimes they will tell you, you provide it, and everyone is happy.

But if you have the depth of knowledge that a *consultant* has, you can make recommendations based on trends that your customers are not yet aware of. You don't want to talk a customer out of a sale by confusing an issue with too many choices, but you should be looking to the future. If you demonstrate that you are on top of the industry customers will call you when they are ready to buy. Can you imagine the impact on your sales if every customer called to ask your opinion before making a purchase? Your competitors would be looking for work very soon.

Knowing your stuff makes selling enjoyable

Knowing your company, industry, customers needs, *your* products as well as your competitors, is not only necessary for success, but leads to job satisfaction as well. Be a constant student of self-improvement, because learning really is a lifelong process. Study selling and marketing as much as you can because trends do change over time.

While you may decide to continue tried-and-true methods that work, it is always good to question the way we do things from time to time. The nature of business changes so rapidly today that chances are you need to change the way you do business. If you do not, you may be missing out on even more business that you think, even if things seem to be going well.

Take the time now to write down five goals you would like to accomplish over the next year. Try to set one goal for each of the five aspects of knowing your stuff. Remember the following rule when setting goals: they should be attainable and measurable. You want to set goals that are a challenge, yet not impossible to reach. Also, it helps to set goals that are measurable so you know when you have reached them.

As an example, a financial planner could set the following goals: Learn more about annuities and the competition's position on them. Learn the trend the industry is following with regard to annuities. How is our company promoting them over other products? What customers are served best by annuities?

A car salesperson could learn more about luxury model features, what cars compete closest to this model, what selling techniques work best, and what is the best target market for this automobile.

Any salesperson in any industry can benefit from this exercise. Take some time. Be creative. Do it now!

My Goals For Knowing My Stuff

1._____

2._____

3._____

4._____

5._____

Compete with yourself

As a closing note, keep in mind that you should compete with yourself instead of other sales people. Measuring your own performance is necessary in order to find areas to improve upon. If you commit to constant improvement, you will be well on your way to success and enjoyment in selling. Competition is healthy to a degree—only if you do not lose sight of your goals and aspirations. Sales contests, quotas, and rankings are useful only if they foster a spirit of teamwork. They often create a spirit of jealousy and resentment that distracts us from reaching our goals.

It is a good idea to look at the *techniques* other successful salespeople use and incorporate these into our daily tactics. However, you must adapt these techniques to fit your own unique personality. You may find it best to adopt different techniques from several different people. Remember, just as you need to learn about your products, industry, and customers, you should strive to out-perform your past results. Constantly improve on your past results and you will grow, achieve, and have a more enjoyable time selling.

Chapter Four

Selling is Selling?

One of the biggest myths alive today is that certain people are "born salespeople." Nothing could be further from the truth; selling can be learned the same as other business skills.

It is important to realize that certain people succeed in different selling environments. There are significant differences between companies, products, and customers. Finding the right fit is critical to job satisfaction and success.

We operate in a global business environment today and that translates into stiff competition for customers. This competition has squeezed prices and hence profits. In the past a salesperson could count on a customer buying a product or service, based on one of three properties; product, price, or service. Customers today demand superior products and services, at low prices, with excellent service. They demand all three elements. In this type of business environment it is necessary that sales people fit well into their company and industry environment.

Hard Sell or Soft Sell?

Individual personalities play an important role in the selling techniques a company chooses to implement. If you know upper management's ideals and philosophies, you will have a good snapshot of what type of directives to expect today and in the future. Do your best to choose a company that matches your own personality. An extroverted personality may teach an outgoing style of selling as the standard for the company. Personality styles are covered in chapter nine.

While individual personalities are difficult to predict in certain businesses, the type of selling required is easier to predict. The *hard sell* and the *soft sell* can be used within the same industry, but generally it is the availability of the customer or prospect that determines which style prevails.

Car selling, for example, is usually a hard sell industry. While it is popular for car dealerships to position themselves as a caring "no hassle" business, most Americans are terrified to buy a car. And for good reason. Stories of car salespeople refusing to return a customer's car keys indicates just one of the many intimidating tactics that have been used by some hard sell car salespeople to prevent the prospect from leaving. Why would a salesperson be so tough on someone? Statistics show that if a car prospect does not buy right then and there, the likelihood of them returning is very slim. This person is not likely to ever be seen again. Therefore, nothing will be lost by pressing hard for the sale.

Most businesses where there is only one opportunity to close the sale utilize the hard sell style. Sales managers in theses types of businesses advocate tactics that get results regardless of the personal feelings of the customer. Health Clubs are another example of businesses that typically utilize the hard sell. Obviously there are some very considerate car dealerships and health clubs in this country, but these are two industries that do more than their share of selling-by-intimidation. In the auto industry we are seeing the result of the consumer demanding a change with the "no dicker sticker" philosophy of the more progressive dealerships.

If money is the one-and-only aspect you desire from your job, the hard sell technique will usually do fine in certain industries. If you hope to have customers as friends, the soft sell is your only choice. No one appreciates being pushed into a buying decision.

Aggressive Tactics vs. Intelligent Persistence

The soft selling style refers to an approach that is very considerate of the customers wants and needs, yet still asserts the benefits of a particular product or service. The method is respectful while assertive, and not aggressive in the traditional sense of the word. Soft selling replaces aggressive tactics with intelligent persistence.

Enthusiasm, sincere listening, product knowledge, and rapport building are the required foundation for soft selling. Finding solutions to your customers problems with your product or service, gaining respect and repeat business, should be the goals.

Since the goal of this book is to help you succeed and enjoy your selling career, the soft sell style would seem to be a prerequisite. Many salespeople resort to the hard sell because it is easier and you don't have to think as much or do your homework. Do not confuse the soft sell with a weak presentation or close. Many people hear the word soft sell and picture a salesperson making a poorly-planned sales call that consists of a casual conversation and no attempt of a close.

We will talk about the critical aspect of closing the sales in the last chapter of this book, but note that the phrase "soft sell" still has the word "sell" in it. An intelligent close must be assertive, and requires some action on the part of the customer.

Being assertive yet respectful is the key to success with this approach. When respect is established between you and the customer, the success rate of closing the sale dramatically increases.

Pick the right horse to ride

Know that there are significant differences between companies and industries. Pick a type of selling that matches your personality. There is a good analogy from horseracing that relates to picking a successful company: Pick the right horse to ride. A good jockey can make a difference, but a good jockey on a mule will never win the Kentucky Derby.

If you require a rapid rise in income to be truly happy, you will not be satisfied with a conservative slow-moving company or industry. Be prepared for a crazy ride with a fast-growing company because rapid growth and change do not occur without tumultuous occurrences. If this situation fits your personality and you are happiest in such a situations, go for it!

Within a certain industry, companies vary greatly with respect to growth prospects. Even in the fast-changing industry of computer software and hardware, some companies are slow-moving. A fast-growing company within a stodgy industry such as banking could possibly be more stimulating than another job in the glittering software industry.

Small privately-owned companies can be a excellent choice to build a career. Large companies provide excellent sales training and are usually a good choice as a first job but there are no hard and fast rules. Selling styles vary, depending on who is at the helm of the sales organization, regardless of the size of the company. With a large company it can be difficult to determine who is calling the shots. A smaller organization can offer the luxury of simplicity; often the sole proprietor sets all the policies. Both large and small companies can offer good compensation, but usually the larger the organization the less potential there is. It can be easier to establish a success record and strong relationship with a small business owner than with a fortune 500 company.

Negotiating a pay raise is rare with the big conglomerates since the rules, regulations, and pay grids leave little room for variation. If a sales manager from a large corporation wants to hire you, there may be only a narrow salary range to make you an attractive offer. Double your sales with a large corporation and you may get noticed and have opportunities for advancement. This is terrific if this is what you want. Doubling your sales with a small company could double your salary and commission and offer the same opportunities in the future.

Many salespeople build successful and enjoyable sales careers with large corporations. Just make sure you don't overlook that small local company that could become the next Microsoft. The personality of the owner/operator makes all the difference in the potential for income and growth. Look hard for a good fit between you and the organization you decide to work for. You owe it to yourself, your family, and your company.

Sales Driven or Market Driven?

The balanced company combines sales and marketing 50/50. The perfectly balanced company only exists in theory, and while some come close, usually one philosophy prevails.

The sales driven philosophy holds that with sales effort and technique, any product or service can be sold. Packaging and promotion is nice, but the real battle is won by salespeople who have the skill and the drive to bring in the business. It is the old "he could sell ice cubes to Eskimos" analogy.

The market driven philosophy contends that if your product or service does not fill a need or want in the market place, you may realize short term sales but long term, growth will be fleeting.

Both philosophies can be valid in certain situations. Certainly in today's marketplace with so many products and services, sales effort is critical. Given similar products and prices, the company with the most driven sales force will usually lead the way. However, the best salesperson in the world may be able to sell yesterday's technology, but for how long? How successful would you be today selling a new computer with a ten-year-old design. This may be an extreme example, but many companies are guilty of this. Many times the reason is the attempt to keep a profitable product or service alive, if not growing, as mentioned in chapter one.

Many times the prevailing philosophy is determined by the background of the person at the helm of the company. A CEO or President with a sales background will often structure the company strategy around the sales philosophy. He or she may allocate a significant part of the budget to the sales department. Conversely a person with a marketing background will emphasize marketing as the primary catalyst to generate sales.

Part Two

Elements of Success

Chapter Five

Attitude—the Framework for Success

Much has been written over the years about attitude. Understanding your attitude is very important in the world of selling where you must communicate and listen effectively. Everyone has mood swings. Learning to recognize them is the first step in the process.

There are many ways to handle slumps in attitude. Recognizing the emotions you are feeling enables you to find a possible solution to the problem. Choosing the right company to work for, and an industry that agrees with your beliefs, is a good start. Even though everyone has bad days, if your personality style does not fit in well with your company or industry, you are likely to have a more difficult time overcoming attitude conflicts. Sales is tough enough on the ego, don't make your job tougher than it should be by choosing a company or industry that is a poor fit to your core values and beliefs. We covered the topic of company style in the previous chapter and we will look at the importance of values and beliefs in Chapter Six.

Make a conscious effort to monitor you thoughts or self-talk

Whoever said that life was a self-fulfilling prophecy was right. Volumes have been written on how we truly do get what we expect in life. If you believe your life is shaped exclusively by your surroundings and environment, you have some work to do. We program our minds with statements of "self-talk" every day. We must make a constant effort to monitor our thought patterns and stop any negative "scripts" as they begin to develop.

Think of all the negative emotions, fear and anger being the most prevalent, as the subject of a video cassette. You have the option to eject this tape whenever and wherever you please. You may want to picture your problem or negative self-talk written on a piece of paper. Visualize crumpling it up, lighting it on fire, and throwing it over a cliff—my personal favorite. This may seem too simple a concept, but as you practice the technique, you will get better at subverting negative thoughts. Negative thinking is dangerous because it is so subtle and powerful. It affects our actions and, hence, outcomes in so many ways. We usually are not aware of this because our subconscious acts automatically, without our approval.

Positive affirmations overcome negativity

There are some keys reasons we slump into poor attitudes. As humans we are creatures of habit and tend to expect what has happened in the past. A good example is calling on customers who have never bought from us before. We tend to psyche ourselves out of a sale because of this fact, and close out any new possibilities.

What happens then? We set up a chain of events to validate

this belief with statements such as, "You don't need to order today, do you?" Of course not, what did you expect?

It is difficult to keep an open mind, but you must try. Any veteran sales professional can tell you a story of customers that *finally* bought at the most unexpected time. We will talk more about affirmations later, but realize that they are specific, quantifiable, positive thoughts.

We have all heard people say "think positive." But getting specific about your positive thinking keeps it consistent with your goals. An affirmation such as, "Today is the day I will get an appointment to see this customer," puts the wheels in motion for success. If you believe it will happen, you instantly become more confident with clear thinking on how to reach this goal. Saying the opposite, "I can never get in to see this customer; it seems hopeless," has the opposite effect on body posture, mannerisms, and even strategy. Our subconscious is powerful and does not want to be proven wrong. If we tell ourselves we will fail, we tend to set the wheels of failure into motion.

Visualize success

Take your positive affirmations one step further—practice visualizing your desired outcome.

Your subconscious mind does not know the difference between an imagined event and the real thing. Have you ever thought of a positive event and felt your body respond with an adrenaline rush? Conversely you can probably recall thinking of something that made you feel anxious and scared.

Focus on visualizing the positive outcome you desire from your selling and personal activities. When you do this you are programing your subconscious to move in this positive direction. Focusing on failures will do the opposite.

The best technique for visualization is to imagine seeing yourself in a selling situation on a television. If you have trouble visualizing yourself, practice selling scenarios with other salespeople in your organization using a video camera. Replaying the scene and watching yourself succeed will certainly help you visualize success later. Also, this is a great way to boost each other's morale.

Visualization is exercise for the brain. Physical exercise is most efficient when it is performed on a regular basis—daily or at least a few times per week. The same goes for positive visualization—make it a goal to practice visualizing success on a regular basis.

Beware of sales call reluctance caused by fear of rejection

Fear of rejection is probably the salesperson's biggest hurdle to overcome. You can get better at dealing personally with rejection, but even old veterans can take only so much of it. Anger and fear are natural instincts left over from our primitive ancestors when the *fight* or *flight* instinct ruled all of our day-to-day actions. Anger and fear will surface any time situations or events trigger *fight* or *flight* reactions.

There are many signs of the fear of rejection, but sales call reluctance (flight) is the most prevalent. Spending too much time on trivial paperwork or other tasks that do not contribute to the outcome of a sale is just one example.

One way to overcome this situation is to make appointments. Many selling situations do not allow this. But often you can nail down even a rough appointment that decreases your chances of being brushed off. With hard-to-see customers, you may not be able to nail down a specific time. Still saying, "I'll be stopping by and would like to see........for less than a minute," can result in a good sales call. "I know Mr./Ms. Smith does not have time to meet, but I want to hand deliver something and then I will be on my way," is another statement that works. Planting a seed often takes less than a minute and you then have something to build on for future calls.

Learn to find humor wherever and whenever you can

Humor is a significant antidote to a negative or counterproductive attitude. Do not underestimate the power of humor. Every day you should make a conscious effort to find humor in something. If you try hard you will find humor where you never did before. It is possible to turn an otherwise frustrating situation into a more tolerable one through humor.

We can all think of situations where, in a group of people, a situation has enraged some while others remain relaxed—under identical conditions. The absurd can be laughable, you may even laugh at yourself for impatience. Perspective helps put things in their proper place and makes it easier to find humor in just about any situation. Remember, everything is relative. If you try hard, you can find good things in situations that seem frustrating. Many times you can even find something funny during these moments.

Cash in on the ability to find humor where none seems to exist when you are having a particularly lousy day. That happens in sales. Some days it seems that every call you make results in a negative comment; you get treated with no respect. Sometimes nothing in your personal life seems to going very well either. Everyone seems to be against you. At these times especially you need to find some humor in the events taking place.

Think of a person or situation that is funny. Perhaps something that happened in the past, or a similar situation that you are in currently reminds you of something funny. It may be as simple as laughing at your own reaction.

It really is ridiculous to take rejection in sales as personal. Learning *not* to take rejection personally takes time; the sooner you learn this skill, the sooner you will enjoy your sales work.

How about some realistic perspective? As a sales person you meet dozens of people every day. These people have their own hopes, fears, problems, and hang-ups. If they treat you poorly, chances are it is not because of you or anything you have done to them. We will talk more about empathy later, but showing some understanding for their situation prevents you from taking their comments personally and helps you move on to building more productive communication and rapport. It is not easy to always be understanding of others. Sometimes getting outside ourselves helps snap us out of the doldrums.

Learn to appreciate what you have in life

Appreciation for what we currently have in our lives helps maintain a healthy positive attitude. Unworthiness and ingratitude rob us of the enjoyment we could otherwise possess. After all, is it not *enjoyment* that we really hope to experience every day of our lives? Unworthiness tells us we are not good enough for what we want, we do not seek it out, and thus do not get it. Ingratitude is the opposite; we believe that what we have is not good enough for us.

Learn to recognize situations where you may be feeling unworthiness and ingratitude. Try your best to replace these with appreciation and gratitude. Appreciation is truly enjoying what you currently possess—material things, relationships, personal traits and qualities. Gratitude is being truly thankful for having been blessed with these things in life.

Make a list right now of all of your blessings, the things that you are thankful for—your health, job, family, etc. Realize that you are wealthy to have of these things. While you may want more, appreciating what you currently have makes you happier than those people constantly chasing the bigger prize. Genuine appreciation and gratitude for all of your blessings, goals and accomplishments leads to peace of mind.

Things that I am grateful for and appreciate in my life:

1. Health_____

_____

2. Family_____

_____

3. Friends_____

_____

4. Job/Career_____

_____

5. Accomplishments_____

_____

6. Plans_____

_____

7. Community_____

_____

No matter what you possess in this world, material or otherwise, you will take them for granted if you do not consciously review them regularly. Do this especially when you are feeling envy, jealousy, or frustration. These destructive negative emotions can be calmed by a simple review of the wealth you already possess. It has been said that wealth is not owning or possessing more, its appreciating what we already have. When you find yourself comparing yourself to others STOP! Take a deep breath and review this exercise.

Find sources of inspiration

Friends, family, churches, community groups, and even printed words can all be sources of inspiration. Tap in to as many sources as you can. An excellent way to keep your attitude in check is to keep positive statements posted where they can be seen daily.

A particular favorite of this author is quoted from *Desiderata*, printed in 1691:

"Go placidly amid the noise and haste, and remember what peace there may be in silence. As far as possible without surrender be on good terms with all persons. Speak your truth quietly and clearly; and listen to others, even the dull and ignorant; they too have their story. Avoid loud and aggressive persons, they are vexations to the spirit. If you compare yourself with others, you may become vain and bitter; for always there will be greater and lesser persons than yourself. Enjoy your achievements as well as your plans. Keep interested in your own career, however humble; its is a real possession in the changing fortunes of time. Exercise caution in your business affairs; for the world is full of trickery. But let this not blind you to what virtue there is; many persons strive for high ideals; and everywhere life is full of heroism. Be yourself. Especially, do not feign affection. Neither be cynical about love; for in the face of all aridity and disenchantment it is perennial as the grass. Take kindly the counsel of the years, gracefully surrendering the things of youth. Nurture strength of spirit to shield you in sudden misfortune. But do not distress yourself with imaginings.

Many fears are born of fatigue and loneliness. Beyond a wholesome discipline, be gentle with yourself. You are a child of the universe, no less than the trees and the stars; you have a right to be here. And whether or not it is clear to you, no doubt the universe is unfolding as it should. Therefore be at peace with God, whatever you conceive Him to be, and whatever your labors and aspirations, in the noisy confusion of life keep peace with your soul. With all its sham, drudgery and broken dreams, it is still a beautiful world. Be careful. Strive to be happy."

Nurture your self-esteem

Self-esteem and attitude are woven together in our personalities. A good way to build self-esteem is to make a commitment to compliment yourself *every time* you do something well. Salespeople have the bad habit of getting down of themselves and this can have a significant negative impact.

Analyze your sales calls and other activities as well, and make a point to tell yourself, "I really did a good job uncovering Mr. Smith's needs and showing how our Gizmo can help him save money." Little comments of "self-talk" add up over time to build a strong self-image and unshakable confidence.

At the same time, red-flag all negative self-talk, which has an equally powerful impact on self-image and can destroy self-esteem and your sales career if not kept in check. When analyzing past events, always look for two things you did well, and one you would like to improve on.

Make a list right now of things you do well. Do not wait. Write down whatever comes to mind whether it is a hobby or job-related. Write them down as affirmations: " I am an excellent negotiator. I am fair and effective. I listen to customers and follow through with all my commitments." Include things you hope to do, or hope to become but have not mastered yet. Again, in the form of affirmations, "I am good with money and pay all my bills on time," even if you need to improve on some area. "I close sales frequently yet am respectful of my customers wishes. I know my products and my industry and am a resource to my customers." Whatever you would like to achieve, write it!

1._____

2._____

3._____

4._____

5._____

6._____

7._____

8._____

9._____

10._____

Once realized, these affirmations can become a tremendous self-esteem builder.

Persistence and enthusiasm maintain a healthy attitude

Persistence and enthusiasm are also integral parts of a person's attitude. You must possess these traits in order to succeed in sales. Do whatever it takes to develop these qualities. Monitor yourself and look for ways to increase persistence and enthusiasm in your day-to-day selling.

Selling something you believe in makes it easy to display honest enthusiasm during your calls. Enthusiasm, in turn, often breeds persistence. When you are genuinely excited about something and expect the customer to buy, you do not give up trying. Try to sell something you believe in so you will not have to fake enthusiasm. Few people can fake enthusiasm over the long run, and even fewer can feel good about doing it. A fake is discovered sooner or later.

Do some soul searching and think about what you truly value in life; this will help you discover a product or service you believe in and can be passionate about. You can certainly find a product or service to sell that is related in some way to your values and beliefs. This true belief in what you are selling gives you sincerity—something many people pick up on and something few people can fake long-term. When you have this foundation, you may have down days, but it will be easier to muster up genuine enthusiasm for what you are selling. Persistence, desire, and effort come to life when you are acting on values you are passionate about. Persistence certainly follows if your actions are based on deeply help values.

As an exercise for future chapters, write down at least four things you value. These can be physical things, personality traits, human qualities, whatever you value deep down inside. They may be work related, but also consider your hobbies and other interests as a source to discover your values.

If you have a hard time doing this spend at least two hours writing about some of your most memorable experiences in life. What were you doing? What were you working with? Information? Machines? People? What was the outcome? This might crystallize some of your deepest values. Take your time; it is not easy. Oftentimes people think back to a sport they were once passionate about and discover that it was not the sport that they loved, but the camaraderie and pursuit of common goals together. Our culture is often so preoccupied with things we feel we *should* do or *should* want that it is easy to forget what we truly care about. Write them down now so you don't forget!

1._____

2._____

3._____

4._____

Even if you are selling a product you absolutely love, you will have days when you are not beaming with sunshine. You may need to make fewer calls on days like that because it is better not to be in front of a customer when you are in a bad mood. Enthusiasm is the quality that lights up your face and creates an aura of excitement all around you. Enthusiasm shows customers that you like your job, your company, and the products you sell. It does, in a sense, pre-sell your product because it sells *you* first.

If you cannot muster up any enthusiasm, spend the day on some productive tasks such as route-planning, administrative tasks, motivational reading, or product knowledge learning. Remember, even the greatest salespeople in the world need to recharge their batteries on a regular basis.

Your daily planner can help you leave your work at the end of the day

One final note for keeping and maintaining a good attitude for selling: leave your work at the end of the day—physically and mentally. Many sales people work out of their homes part-time or full-time. The temptation to work throughout the evening and weekend is great indeed. You may consider it *dedicated* to read memos or do other work on Saturday. If you burn out, everyone loses—you, your company, and your customer.

Schedule time so that you control events, not the other way around. Certainly there are times when you have to work after-hours, but do your best to maintain balance in your life. Thinking about your work is the same as doing it or being there as far as your mind is concerned. Your daily planner can assist you here. If you write everything down, nothing falls through the cracks. If you do not complete all the tasks on your "to-do today" list, write them in tomorrow's box or under the appropriate day some time in the future. We will talk about this critical organization tool later in the book.

A one-dimensional person's job is their entire life. This type of person is not very interesting to anyone, customers included. Work hard to develop a variety of outside interests for the good of your own well-being and career. Resentment and burnout are just around the corner if the job runs your life. Put the stack of sales figures that came in the Saturday mail aside for your late Sunday or early Monday planning. Remind yourself frequently that your time off is mandatory for "charging your batteries."

Chapter Six

Planning and Goal Setting

Goals are the beginning of an action plan

Before getting into concepts to assist you in planning and goal setting, it is important to address the reasons why you need to do it. We all know we should plan, but often we don't do it because "more important" things seem to come up. Writing your goals down on paper, and keeping them available for constant review and update, is the only way to prevent forgetting what you really want to accomplish with your time.

However, you can get carried away and become so goal-driven that you forget to enjoy the process of working toward your endeavor. You may even forget the original reason you set the goal. Goals can be changed based on new information. Do not become too rigid in adhering to what you have committed to paper. Goals are an excellent guideline to follow, but many times we decide to accomplish them in a different way, based on new information. Written-down goals serve another valuable purpose: to help you appreciate what you have, and prove that you are getting where you want to go.

Written goals build self esteem

All of us have a tendency to discount what we accomplish. When we look back on goals written down in the past, we realize that we are achieving what we set out to do. If we do not have this reference source, we tend to fall into a trap of always wanting more and saying things like, "Yeah, this is a nice house, but a larger one would be better," or, "that was a pretty good sale, but I should have sold him XYZ as well."

Sometimes sales managers or supervisors foster this feeling of "never enough" by trying to improve on an already good result. There is nothing wrong with improving on a good result *unless* we forget to compliment ourselves on a job well done, or we discount past accomplishments! What we should be saying to ourselves is, "I reached my goal of owning my own home. It took me a year or two longer than I thought it would, but I am proud of myself. Now my goal is a larger house in a nicer neighborhood." Or, "I did a great job selling our product to that account. My persistence and knowledge paid off. I will grow this account even more with other product lines."

It is important to think big in order to achieve our best, but when we discount significant accomplishments already achieved, we undermine our self-esteem and happiness. Some people believe that never being satisfied is a good thing because it leads to improvement. Try to balance the tendency toward complacency with that of perfection. Sometimes "good enough" is just that and perfection is overkill. Pat yourself on the back regularly for goals you have attained.

Count your blessings

Not enough can be said about taking time to appreciate what

you have in life. Enjoy your achievements as well as your plans. You deserve it. How is your health? If it is good or even average you have something money cannot buy. It has been said that money can buy medicine, but not health. How are your friendships and relationships with family and loved ones? If you have just one true friend you have something money cannot buy. Friendships take time and an investment of caring and concern. Money can buy acquaintances, but not true friends.

Practice enjoying what you currently possess, whether possessions, health, or relationships. If you look hard, you can find some real wealth in your life. Look back on the list you created in the last chapter and add to it.

Stress-free goals

Goals are meant to help you enjoy life not stress you out. It might be beneficial to label your goals "expectations." Many people believe that goals should have strict deadlines that *must* be met, no matter what. This may be the reason many people avoid setting goals in the first place. This kind of pressure can take the enjoyment out of life. If you are having this problem use the word *expectations* instead of *goals*.

If you expect to have a bigger house within the next five years, and set smaller intermediate goals to work towards this end, you are laying a foundation to succeed. Do not be too concerned about meeting deadlines. If you are working toward several goals at the same time some will happen sooner and some later. In the long run, the average works out to *achievement*. Give yourself credit for something many people never do—set goals in the first place. Simply setting goals and working toward them at any pace puts you well ahead of the average person. If fear of failure keeps you from setting goals, remember—you cannot stumble if you stand still but you cannot get anywhere unless you move.

Believing that you have failed by not reaching the exact deadline implies you can control every event in your life. Many self-improvement books teach that you are in control of your life, and that circumstances do not determine your achievements. This is true to a certain extent; you must take control and know that *you* have the greatest impact on what you will achieve in life. You really do get what you expect from life because of the subtle subconscious programming that goes on in your mind day after month after year.

However, there are forces in the universe you cannot control. Certainly you can make bad situations better by the way you react, but if your company goes out of business you probably will not achieve some of your goals as scheduled. If this happens change the date on the goals or change the goals to reflect the new information. Take it in stride because many things in this life rely on the actions of other people. We truly cannot do it all ourselves. Coworkers and family members can have a huge influence on the outcome of projects we undertake. It is usually a good idea to keep goals and expectations more general if people are involved in the process. People mean well, but they do not always have your interests at the top of their mind.

Much is written on the importance of planning and goal-setting with regard to *what to say* and *who to see*. Based on your company's goals you need to have a strategy before you develop a call cycle, and a priority of what to talk about. But you should not let this be your *only* guiding light. You should have goals and expectations for *every* major part of your life: career, family, physical/health, community and spiritual. You may even consider breaking each of these down into subcategories. Much of the dissatisfaction we face in our work and personal lives is caused because we allow events into our lives that conflict with our core beliefs and values.

Your goals should incorporate your values

The type of goal setting that leads to the greatest success, both financially and spiritually, is that which incorporates your deepest values. When your daily activities are in line with your deeply-held values, you will truly be a happy person.

Ask yourself, "Are my actions based upon my chosen values, upon my mood, or upon circumstances?" Write a one-paragraph mission statement that spells out what you want your life to stand for. Think of what you would want your eulogy to be. In order to insure proper direction, ask yourself if your actions flow from your mission. Use these written values to determine goals, then carry over these goals into daily activities. You must write down your values and goals (expectations) in life if you are ever to achieve them.

It has been said over and over again, "If you fail to plan, you plan to fail." If you do not have a direction in life, any course will do. This is so true. Use the exercises you complete in this book to create goals for your daily planner. Think of these exercises as a "first draft" of your goals and values with the final version going into your planner system. This way you can review them daily, change and add to them as required.

There are many excellent daily planner systems available today. Choose one that can be customized in a way that you *use* it. In Chapter Five you wrote down some values you cherish. You may want to revisit your notes from that chapter and spend some time with your daily planner. If you have a problem with procrastination, schedule a two-hour block of time *now* in your daily planner to complete this task.

Organization is a requirement for effective planning

Effective planning begins with good organization. Organization can help reduce anxiety in your life—at work and in the home. If you know where you are going, and have a solid plan before you venture out, you can avoid the frustration of "spinning your wheels." When your work life is in order, you are able to enjoy yourself at home knowing that your work is under control.

Realize the significant role that planning plays in your overall ability to control events in your life, and you will be well on your way to job satisfaction. Basic organization includes job related *and* personal organization. Some people are very organized at work and a mess in their personal life, but this is more the exception than the rule. There are some fundamental organization techniques that will help even the most unorganized person improve in this area.

The first step is to recognize the areas of your life that could be improved by better organization. You do not have to have all your shirts organized by color in your closet to improve the quality of your life. If you spend a half-hour in the morning trying to *find* your shirts, this is an area that needs better organization. Looking at all areas of your personal and work life will probably reveal some time-wasting methods of doing things. We all are creatures of habit and tend to stick to the old ways whether or not they make sense.

There are three basic areas that sales people tend to get bogged down in: the desk, the car, and the appointment book (daily planner). Let's look at these three areas and recognize possible improvements.

Most sales people do not give much thought to managing their desk. After all, most selling is not done over the phone. The desk seems to be a place to dump all those memos and return phone calls. That's it. A properly-organized desk is a real time-saver. Conversely, a sloppy desk is a time-waster.

Consider the problem of mail. When your mail comes in, do you open it, read through it, and pile it up for more than a day? Most people do, and therefore create more work for themselves later on. If you open your mail, read it, then stack it, you will have to deal with it again later.

Your goal should be to handle every piece of paper in your life *once*. There is no need to have papers on your desk, although some people do it so they look busy. As a sales professional, you are lucky to be judged on results and not how many hours you put in or how busy you look. Mail is one of the few controllable events in your life. Phone calls and interruptions are more difficult to manage than mail. So take advantage of this and control the mail so it does not control you.

Since many sales professionals work out of the home, at least part-time, there is no separating personal and business organization. All the mail comes together so that organization in personal affairs carries over to the job. When you open your mail, you should read each piece and make a decision what to do with it. The best option is probably to throw it away. If there is something important to act on, write it down in your daily planner according to the time frame required. For example, if you receive a notice about a CD renewing, write the account number under the day it is to renew, toss out the paper and forget about it.

You might get a letter from a long-lost friend with a new phone number. He says he will be back in town in three weeks and hopes to get together. Jot down the new number in your address section of your planner and also make a note three weeks from now to call him. We will talk more about the daily planner and how closely it is linked to everything regarding time management, planning and organization.

Your next option is to file the paper for future reference. Not all matters in your business and personal life can be managed with a few notes and a phone number. Company memos, insurance policies, bank statements, product information, all need to be retained for future reference. Do not get carried away; do you really need to save those bank statements for over one year? Maybe, maybe not, but make sure you think before you hoard. Saving receipts from purchases is a good idea, especially if the item is expensive and meant to last awhile.

The daily planner is your link to organizing all the events that happen in your life. A few filing cabinets and your daily planner are all it takes to have a clear desk. You can file everything. If you have a hard time finding a category for less obvious pieces of paper, file under the label, "Stuff I don't know what to do with." You may want to create a file folder labeled "Holding Pen" to file all the things you used to keep on your desk that require ongoing reference. These may be things you have already acted on but are not comfortable tossing in the "round file" quite yet. At a later date you can decide on a special place for these notes and memos. If you need to act on a memo in the future, simply make a notation in your daily planner on that future date. A desk full of memos, letters, and stick-em notes is not the best way to manage things. Commit to file folders, your daily planner notes, and the trash can, and you will have a neater desk and a more organized life.

The daily planner is your best organization tool

We have talked about the daily planner in this and other parts of the book, but more needs to be said about this critical organizational tool. The main purpose of any daily planning system is to organize time in order to control *activities* and *occurrences*. Try to think of control in a positive way. Control includes deciding *not* to control certain things at all. Many occurrences cannot be controlled, but can be prevented with good planning and organization. Managing activities is an area that you do have the most control over.

It all comes down to being realistic about what you can achieve in a limited amount of time. Realize there are activities you *can* control but believe you cannot. Likewise there are activities you *cannot* control but think you can. Learn to recognize things you have no control over and those with which you have total control. Opening mail is an activity you can control.

We *choose* to do things in the category of activities that we have total control over while we *conform* to those activities and occurrences over which we have no control. As a sales rep you may find yourself working too much, but you *choose* to open that company mail on Sunday. It's hard not to, especially if you know your quota achievement is in there. None-the-less, you have control over this activity. There are many activities we must conform to: mandatory paperwork, meetings, and various people and situations.

Remember that most things in life are a choice and there are few things you *must* do. We choose to do many of the things we think we have to do because the alternative of facing the consequences is worse than the event itself. Your manager may call a mandatory meeting; while you may not get fired for refusing to attend, the potential consequences to your career make attending the wise choice.

"Must do" vs. "Should do" activities and occurrences

Emergencies, last minute appointments, and critical deadlines— are difficult, if not impossible, to control. A top customer threatens to terminate their relationship unless you stop by at noon. A loved one is rushed to the hospital with a serious injury. These occurrences take priority over everything else. You do choose to act on emergencies, but morally as a human being, you *must* act on them. Unnecessary phone calls and interruptions, meaningless paperwork, gossip, and other unproductive activities are neither a "must do" or a "should do" event.

Should do activities consist of planning, education, job skill learning, relationship building and needed leisure. We should spend most of our time in this area, but most people tend to get stuck in the other less productive activities. One key area is that of prospecting for new customers and managing accounts and territories. All types of industries require sales people to prospect for new customers. If you are in real estate or insurance, prospecting must be a major part of your daily goals. Regardless of the industry, you will lose customers and you must replace them in order to increase your business incrementally.

Who should you call on? How often? What products or services should you emphasize? To Whom? How can you get new customers? How can you get more sales out of existing customers? All of these questions should be answered before you hit the road to make a sales call.

The following technique for planning has proven to be successful over the years. In the evening before or in the early morning, set aside fifteen minutes to plan your day. Review your values and goals and try to incorporate smaller related goals into your daily activities. At the very least, work them into your monthly goals. The goals should include personal ones as well as the obvious business goals. Sales people working for a particular company should plan calls based on the company strategy and stick to it as best as possible. Don't be too hard on yourself if you need to divert from your plan. The fact that you have written out a call plan should help keep you from deviating.

Consider your customers needs when planning strategy

Based on your company strategy you will have to decide who to call on each day. If you are a company representative with an exact account list, your planning task will be easier than if you are an insurance agent, real estate agent, financial planner, or small company representative. For company representatives of larger corporations you will probably be given a mandate on which accounts to call on and how often. You may also have a formalized strategy per month, quarter, or year depending on your business. Remember as mentioned in Chapter Two, your management has good intentions when they design selling strategy, but do not let this blind you to customer requirements. There are always exceptions and you will have customers that ask to be called on in a different manner than you are told.

Who do you listen to? Your customer is your livelihood and if you develop a bad relationship you have damaged something very valuable for the long term. Relay all the information you can to management about special situations, but take it upon yourself to manage your customers. This is why salespeople cannot be replaced by technology. Customers differ from each other, and good salespeople are able to adapt and customize selling strategy based on these differences. If selling could be automated and standardized, companies could utilize a robot sales force instead of people.

Many company representatives sell to a specialized market. Prospecting is somewhat limited to a specific industry or business. Selling more products to existing customers is usually the way to increase sales in this type of environment. Pharmaceutical, consumer, industrial, medical, and institutional sales are just a few industries that have a very focused customer base.

Insurance, real estate, and financial representatives have a more challenging job prospecting and managing accounts. While these professionals can also concentrate on selling more products to existing customers, the attrition rate of current customers is usually greater. Cold calling and a whole array of guerrilla marketing techniques are required to increase sales. Successful real estate and insurance agents are masters at using local newspaper ads, community projects, mailing, and networking with every warm body they meet, to market themselves and the service they provide.

Have a mission

Every day, make it a point to have two or three things that you want to accomplish in addition to your routine activities. Sometimes this is referred to as *targeting* your customers. Think of something you would like to accomplish: perhaps getting into to see a difficult customer, or selling a new product to an existing account. Smaller goals always help to make an apparently large task that seems impossible suddenly seem more realistic. Have some kind of impact every day.

Chapter Seven

Personal Time and Meditation

While there is no substitute for hard work, this alone will not lead to success or satisfaction in the sales profession. Working hard at working *smart* is a better strategy than simply working hard. Many authors of selling tips and techniques proclaim that the person that gets up at five a.m. and works weekends is bound to succeed. Certainly for some people this is a formula for success. But others have burned out and failed with the same formula.

There is no standard prescription for success and satisfaction in sales. If you have truly absorbed what Chapter Five has emphasized about attitude, you will know what you need to do to take care of yourself. While it is important in any line of work, selling requires more "charge your battery" time than most professions. Even the strongest egos get bruised. If you accept this fact, you will bounce back from disappointments quickly and enjoy selling much more. Remember that you are a unique person with needs that no one else has.

Listen to your moods and your body. If your neck and back are stiff and you are anxious and irritable, these are signals that your day-to-day activities are going against something you truly believe. You may be neglecting some core needs. Try changing your routine somehow. Even small changes, such as updating your selling materials and binders can put a new twist on your day. You may need to change your call schedule or the way you go about selling. This does not always work, but is worth trying and could be the start of a search for positive changes. If it takes something this small to help you out of a slump you are lucky.

Change is good, so if you are restless, look for ways to change your daily activities and implement them. It is beneficial to periodically question the way you are doing things and the reasons why. Frequently, individuals and companies get stuck in outdated ways of conducting business. Make sure your methods and techniques change appropriately with the times. Try everything you can think of. Don't give up.

Take good care of yourself—Do not kill the goose for the golden egg

Call it meditation, personal time, or veg time, but the purpose is the same. Sales can be hectic when you consider the opposing forces of your customer and your company. You often feel pulled in two different directions as though you are about to come apart at the joints. Combine this with being stuck in traffic and you have a great combination for a nervous breakdown.

You need to take care of yourself. Find your center and do something nice for yourself. Some type of exercise that helps you clear your mind is terrific and can prevent you from reacting to the stresses of the day. Whether you use the martial arts,

Tai Chi, Yoga, jogging, or any variation and combination of activities, everyone needs an outlet. Make sure you choose one that is healthy to body, spirit and mind.

Aesop tells a story of a king who had a goose that laid golden eggs. In an effort to get the most golden eggs out of the goose, the king overworked and neglected the goose. He forgot to balance the care for the asset that produced the output, and focused on the end result. He eventually destroyed the goose, and hence the capacity to produce what he wanted.

You must do whatever it takes to maintain your capacity and earning potential. Only you can learn what this is. Since you are not a machine, it will be different from somebody else. Listen to your body and try to understand your emotions, especially during times of anxiety. No one knows better than you what it takes to maintain and improve yourself. You are an important asset in the productive sense and also in the human sense. You have earning potential but also the capacity to care for others.

You may want to try some on the following as ways to charge your batteries.

Find a Mentor

An excellent way to keep perspective is to find a mentor to whom you can talk to regularly. A person outside your company, not threatened in any way by your success, and not overly judgmental, is ideal. Such a person is not easy to find. Attending selling seminars and conventions is a great way to meet such people. (People within your company could possibly use things you say against you in the future.) Most sales managers do not respect people that complain, and, let's face it, sometimes we need to vent a little steam. Unless they have been in sales, family and friends are not as objective or knowledgeable about what you are going through on the job.

Take a day off

Take a vacation day and do something you have wanted to do for a long time. It is well established that formal vacations create a lot of stress and anxiety before, during and after. There's the planning, the travel, and the money spent. Getting up one morning and deciding to take a spontaneous day off can be a real attitude adjuster. Force yourself to try some things you have never done before. If you are a constant mover, like most salespeople are, go to a park and meditate for a few hours. We all need contrast in our lives to keep things in perspective.

Attend a motivational seminar

This is a great way to improve your outlook. Action and ideas are the things that move us out of ruts. While some of us get a little bored at an all-day seminar, there are shorter workshops and courses on public speaking offered in communities everywhere. You can even attend your own personal seminar by listening to an entire audio cassette program or reading a great book.

Go on a job interview

Make it a point to go on one or two job interviews a year for positions you find interesting. You may find a better position than the one you currently have. At the very least, you will improve your interviewing skills. You may learn that your current job is better than anything available and may therefore dedicate more effort to your current position. The interview may provide the valuable perspective that prevents you from making a poor career move. Sales people, as a rule, are inquisitive. It is natural to wonder if the grass is greener on the other side. Go take a look. Then decide to get on with the job search or put the restlessness behind you and get on with your job.

Exercise regularly, eat a well-balanced diet, and get enough sleep

This may sound like a cliché, but it has a large impact on your happiness in both your personal life and career. You do not have to be an exercise fanatic. Walking briskly for 30 minutes three to four times a week can add years to your life. Making a conscious effort to eat some fruits and vegetables each day and drinking enough water will make you feel much better than eating whatever is convenient. Getting the right amount of sleep can keep you looking vibrant and help you enjoy the day. Of course, we cannot always do these things, but if we commit to making them priorities and personal goals, they will occur more often.

Chapter Eight

Human Aspects

Listening skills and empathy are the key to building quality relationships

How can you demonstrate to your customers that you care about them without good listening skills? This is one area everyone can improve upon. No matter how well you listen, if you are a sales professional you are always tempted to talk a customer to death.

As salespeople, we are encouraged to do this with suggestions, memos, and training, all instructing us to tell the customer what our product can do for them. This is called "My Product" selling. This type of selling is the typical sales pitch customers are all to familiar with and dread. *Feature-benefit* selling is the standard technique taught in many seminars and selling books and is a specific form of "My Product" selling.

Selling on features and benefits does not truly uncover what the customer needs and does nothing to raise you to the resource status you desire. Feature-benefit selling goes something like this: "Ms. Jones, our gizmo has high speed capacity (feature), which means you can print twice as fast (benefit)." What if Ms. Jone's current speed is more than satisfactory? She may benefit more from a higher quality printing.

As a professional salesperson you should also be a professional *listener*. This caliber of listening goes beyond the physical act of closing your mouth and hearing what the other person is saying. It includes the difficult task of interpreting between the lines in order to find out what the customer wants. Most customers will not come out and tell you exactly what they want; oftentimes this is because they do not even know. The issue of asking the right questions is addressed in Part Three of this book. This is just an example to show you the danger of this type of technique. Selling this way will categorize you as a "typical salesperson," a title you cannot afford to have bestowed upon you.

How well do you listen? A good test is to consciously monitor what percentage of the time during your sales call *you* do the talking. Do this just for one day. If you talk more than 50% of the time, you are probably talking too much and involving the customer too little. It is not unusual for sales people to talk 90% of the time. How can you uncover a customers needs and find out their concerns if you are talking? It is no surprise that many customers avoid sales people. Learn to talk less and listen more and you will find doors opening up for you.

Empathy in selling means more than simply putting yourself in your customers shoes. While this is a start, you have to really care about their business and personal needs. You must be confident that if you help people get what they want, you will in turn get what you want—the sale. You do have to care about their concerns before you can expect a return down the road.

Sometimes you have to be patient since this may take longer than you expect. It is much like putting wood in a fireplace. You wouldn't sit in front of a fireplace on a cold day and say, "Come on, give me some heat!" Investing time with your customers shows empathy towards them and is much like fueling a fire. When you care deep down inside you trigger creative solutions that are unavailable to salespeople who don't really care. It comes back again to establishing a "win-win" relationship. Life is not a zero sum game with only so many pieces of pie to go around. The market pie grows larger for those who are willing to invest time and concern helping customers meet their needs.

Integrity and commitment—Do what you say you will do

Do your actions follow your words? In other words do you "walk the talk?" Sales people have been known through the ages to exaggerate and lay the b...s.... on pretty thick. The qualities of integrity and commitment separate sales professionals from the rest of the pack.

Honest enthusiasm is expected of you by your customers; they even anticipate a little "inflation" when it comes to talking up your product or service. Do not get carried away. Do not make small promises you do not intend to keep, such as, "we really should get together for lunch sometime." If you say this often and never do it, you are creating an image in your customers mind of someone who does not follow through. If you say it, you should be ready to schedule it. Do not give insincere compliments. Learn the skill of uncovering good qualities in people so you can give *sincere* compliments.

Do not attempt to gloss over the truth when it comes to products or services. Today's customers are more intelligent and informed that those of past generations. Accurate consumer information is widely available through newspapers, TV and magazines. The truth is important so you can feel good about yourself at the end of the day, and your integrity is not compromised. Lack of integrity has ended more than one promising sales career.

Sometimes salespeople take it upon themselves to change a customers original order because of backorders or production problems. This can destroy your credibility and your company's by earning a reputation for shipping things not ordered. You may consider doing this for fear that the customer will cancel the order altogether if you cannot ship exactly what they want. The risk is not worth it when you consider the damage an irate customer can do to your reputation. The small amount of time it takes for a phone call is well spent.

Honesty is a cornerstone, and make sure you add substance to your presentation. Your goal should be to keep your customers interested in what you have to say. It is not honest to say or imply you have something important to see a customer about and then waste their time with a repetitive presentation.

For your personal well-being and career longevity, honesty is the best policy. It is not worth ruining your reputation with small untruths. A $10 discrepancy on an expense report can mark you as a person that is dishonest. It is not the $10 that matters, but the fact that there was a dishonest act, whether it was on purpose or not. Quickly clear up any misunderstanding; not saying anything makes you appear guilty. If you make a mistake in a matter, address it immediately.

Image is important, but people are usually judged by their

actions and deeds over time. Often times it is better not to draw attention to some things. While it may seem like lying by omission, bringing up every little detail can become tiresome for your superiors. They will appreciate you taking some responsibility on your own. Just make sure you are clear in what areas you are allowed to have discretion.

Under-promise, over-deliver

Most sales people over-promise and under-deliver. Always do the opposite; *under-promise* and *over-deliver*. One common question that can create good will or ill will is, "When can we expect the shipment?" Be very careful how you answer. If you tell a customer that they will receive a shipment in one week and it takes nine days, you have lied to them. Many customers have been deceived in the past by salespeople, so they watch for these little inconsistencies.

If they ask "When will the shipment come?" before you answer, ask if there is a need to rush the order. Often they are simply curious as to when to expect the shipment. Even if there is no rush to get the product, they still monitor what you promise. If it should take one week to ship the product, tell them, "It usually takes one week to ten days to deliver the product to your door. We can rush it for you if you are in urgent need." This shows real concern and demonstrates that you are the type of person who will work for them. Many times their response is, "No rush; I was just curious." Be careful that you do not make a bad situation out of nothing by what you say or even do not say to your customers.

Follow-through and followup

Follow through with what you say you will do—and then followup. Of course you need to follow through when you say you will place an order or service an account problem. But do not forget the importance of the details. Many salespeople think a customer will not remember a small promise. Any veteran salesperson knows that customers tend to remember the *smallest* details. They are better than elephants sometimes. If you promise to send a copy of a certain report, and forget, they write you off as a "typical salesperson." If you promise something that is small and follow through, even if they have forgotten about it, they will be very impressed with your commitment and follow through. You score extra points as a sales person with integrity and stand out from the rest of the crowd. What a great thing to accomplish.

After a customer receives an order, call or stop by to check and make sure everything is going well with the product or service. This followup serves many important functions; it prevents a small problem from exploding into a big one, shows genuine sincerity, demonstrates good organization skills, and, proves your integrity as a sales professional. All of that for a few minutes on the phone or a quick sales call.

Many customers who order products that are technical, and even those that are not, require quite a bit of coaching. They may have forgotten how to use your product by the time it is shipped.

This chapter ends Part Two—Elements of Success. While Part Two covered aspects that influence the actions of you as a salesperson, Part Three—Elements of Selling, emphasizes the customer.

Part Three

Elements of Selling

Chapter Nine

Understanding Different Personalities

The key to understanding others is knowing ourselves first

Much has been written about different personality styles. Models are created in an attempt to categorize personality styles and can make understanding them easier. They are rarely 100% accurate when applied to everyone, but are better than nothing at all. Some models are very specific and others tend to be general. Keep an open mind when applying any model or framework to individual people, and try not to think in absolutes.

The first step in understanding the personalities of others is learning to understand your own. This can be tough for some people, so it is best to solicit the help of an unbiased party. You may want to pick someone that is not too close to you for this exercise. Close friends and family can be biased and will more-than-likely be afraid of hurting your feelings with the truth. Pick an honest person who knows you well enough to have seen you in different situations. The more forthright the better. Ask the following questions of at least two or more people who have known you well during the past several years:

How would you describe my personality in general?
Do you consider me more outgoing or more introverted?
Do you consider me more detail-oriented, practical, or happy-go-lucky?
More independent than most people? or a real group lover?
A fast or slow decision maker?

This information means nothing by itself, but taken together with what you will learn in this chapter and your own self-knowledge, can add to understanding your personality.

The four personality traits

There are four traits that define a person's personality style:
- Logical vs. Intuitive
- Introverted vs. Extroverted

Think of these four not as absolutes but in degrees on a continuum. Some people are clearly Introverted—keeping to themselves and shying away from large group activities. Others seem to be more Extroverted—thriving in a group environment. Both personalities can be good salespeople and good customers. Many people combine the traits of Logic and Intuition, but most are usually more one than the other. Usually people fall completely on the right or left of each of the four traits.

Displaying these four traits on a graph helps grasp the concept of personality styles. On the horizontal axis Introverted is on the left and Extroverted is on the right. On the vertical axis Logical is on the top and Intuitive is on the bottom.

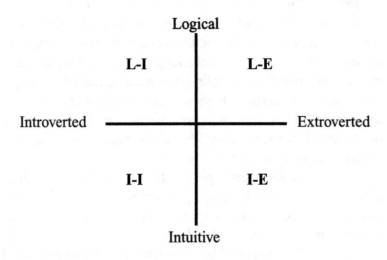

The Logical-Introverted (L-I) personality is non-communicative and a slow-decision maker. This person may stare off into space while you are talking. They are probably listening and analyzing every word you say. They are very detail-oriented and process all the information you give them. They will usually ask for more information than you are able to provide them, so make sure you followup after the sales call. When selling to this type of personality you must have all your facts straight down to the last detail. L-I personalities are not moved by emotions as a primary reason for buying. For this reason they are sometimes the most difficult personality to sell. Once sold they can be the most loyal customers. If you are this type of personality you should be selling highly technical products or services.

Intuitive-Introverted (I-I) Personalities tend to consider themselves primarily when making a purchasing decision. They are not as interested in the outside world and what other people are doing and are also slow decision makers. They are concept-oriented and trust their gut feelings when making decisions. Logical reasons for making a buying decision are not as important as feeling and emotion. Indifference sometimes appears to be the nature of this personality. The solution to this is to get them involved through questions.

Both of the Introverted personality styles have some similarities. They tend to be stoic by nature and are not outwardly passionate about the decisions they make. If they are excited about something you usually don't know it by their outward reactions. In their personal life they tend to prefer solo or small group activities over large group activities. Contemplation and quiet thought dominate their decision-making methods.

The Logical-Extroverted (L-E) personality wants just the facts and very little small talk and socializing. They buy when it makes sense for practical business reasons and are pragmatic in most areas of their lives. A more emotional customer will buy because of the feelings they get from the product. We all buy for emotional reasons and the Logical-Extroverted customer is influenced by emotion, but this personality must justify the purchase *logically* as well.

Intuitive-Extroverted customers can be sold simply because everyone else has bought the product and it looks and sounds great. They want to fit in with the crowd and not be left behind. They are expressive, assertive, outwardly passionate about the decisions they make, and will not nit-pick about the details. For this reason they are often the easiest personality to sell to. If it sounds good, looks good on paper and you appear to be good for your word, they will probably buy. Unfortunately they are likely to buy from others just as easily, so are not always the most loyal customers.

The Introverted personalities on the left-hand side tend to be stoic in nature. The Extroverted personalities on the right-hand side tend to be expressive and outwardly passionate about their ideas. The Logical personalities on the top tend to be detail-oriented. The Intuitive personalities on the bottom tend to be concept-oriented.

Take some time now to answer the following questions for yourself. You may already know what type of personality you are, but the answers to these questions may reveal some important aspects of your personality that you are not aware of.

1. At a sports event or business seminar, are you quickly bored, wishing you could just catch the last half or have the notes from the meeting sent to you? If so, you are probably a Logical-Extroverted personality.

2. Do you thrive in a group setting, love the excitement of large events, hate details and trust your gut feeling to make quick decisions? These are characteristics of the Intuitive-Extroverted personality.

3. When faced with decisions, do you find yourself digging up as many facts as you can to arrive at a decision? If you enjoy information, detail, and have strong powers of concentration, you fall into the Logical-Introverted group of personalities.

4. Do you enjoy keeping to yourself or a small close-knit group of people, trust your hunches more than facts, and hate overly-hyped-up personalities? These are characteristics of the Intuitive-Introvert.

Nothing is clear cut and dried when it comes to personalities. While every person has a combination of the different styles in their make-up, one usually prevails. The purpose of asking others their opinions and combining that knowledge with your own, is to get the clearest, most objective picture of something that is complicated by its nature.

Customize your selling style to the customer's personality

Traditional sales training teaches that you must have enthusiasm when you sell. Many books and training systems imply or openly state that if you have enthusiasm you can make up for lack of product knowledge or other information. While enthusiasm is a key ingredient to move a customer toward a sale, this trait alone cannot launch you into consultant or resource status.

Intuitive-Extroverted customers respond best to a "traditional" ultra-enthusiastic selling approach. They love a high-energy sales presentation, expect the whole show, and will probably be disappointed if they do not get it. Intuitive-Extroverted people are usually driven by emotion and concepts vs. logic and detail. They may decide to buy your product before asking you the price. If you have a sound idea that makes sense, they will usually give it a try.

Logical-Introverted personalities are the direct opposite of the Intuitive-Extrovert. These two personalities can drive each other crazy. The Logical-Introvert is a slow decision maker. Non-communicative and detail-oriented, they are not impressed by hype and want plenty of information to provide them with a basis for understanding the problem at hand.

With the Logical-Extroverted customer, don't spend too

much time on small talk. Get down to business. Have a sound proposal, and you have a great chance of establishing a relationship. These people are assertive and interested in details only to a degree, and are very practical in all their affairs.

The Intuitive-Introverted personality is concept-oriented and stoic in nature, another non-communicative personality, but more emotional. Their feelings and intuition come into play when making a buying decision. Give this person the time and space they need to make a decision. Take your time, be patient, and you have a good chance of establishing a long-term relationship.

This model for categorizing personalities is only a rough sketch. Use the above information in *addition* to common sense and other information learned from interacting with your customers. Treat every customer as the individual they are, with their own set of beliefs and paradigms that were established over years of unique upbringing. It is no surprise that most salespeople sell the best to people that are like themselves.

Use this model and practice relating to as many different personality styles as you can. Anywhere you go—the repair shop, grocery store, restaurant—practice interacting with different personalities. Coworkers and colleagues are a good source as well. Think of it as a game, trying to figure out which type of personality people are. Then practice effective communication with each type.

As you may have guessed, some professions are composed of one or two predominant personality styles. Engineers, dentists, and physicians are just a few of the more Logical-Introverted professions. Professionals in large bureaucratic agencies and businesses, teachers, and educators tend to be composed more of Intuitive-Introverted personality types. The Logical-Extroverted personality fits the stereotype of the entrepreneur or classic business person. Salespeople tend to be typically Intuitive-Extroverted personalities. As mentioned before, personalities sell best to those that are like themselves.

You will sell more and enjoy the process if you can relate to a wide group of varied personality types. It helps to be somewhat of a chameleon and match your mannerisms to that of the customer. Customers like to buy from people they are like. This does not mean being fake. It merely means adapting to a situation by expressing different parts of your personality.

Everyone has parts of the four distinct personality traits described above. Some may think of it as acting. Good actors actually bring up real, often painful, experiences to get into a specific role they are playing. It is well-established that merely thinking of something pleasant can change the body's metabolism. So try your best to be energetic with the Extroverted personalities, understanding with the Introverted, detail-oriented with the Logical, and concept-oriented with the Intuitive.

If you sell a product or service to people in different economic groups, there is an entirely new dimension to the above model. There is a wide variation in the way people of different socioeconomic groups view life and its processes. If you are selling a product or service to a mechanic or a plumber, your approach should match the conditions and environment they work in.

Customers who roll up their sleeves and get dirty for a living can get irritated or offended by a person who is too polished. In their view they feel talked down to, that the salesperson is above them. A more straight-forward sales approach may work more effectively with these individuals. If you do not diffuse negative feelings, it is impossible to move towards establishing a productive business relationship. Again, it makes sense to be somewhat of a chameleon and imitate your environment. Save the polished presentation for the white collar customers who expect it. There are some exceptions, and certainly you will find analytical or extroverted people in all types of work. But recognize that there are similarities unique to every segment of both white and blue collar occupations.

When making small talk and establishing rapport, use the information revealed during conversation to help understand a person. An Extroverted personality will often play in a tennis league or on a golf team, will talk enthusiastically and shake your hand firmly. Customize your approach and presentation to fit this type of personality. If you practice this process consciously for one month, it will become a habit and you will be able to figure out fairly quickly what makes people tick. Besides, it is fun to do. You learned about empathy in previous chapters; understanding others is critical to developing empathy with your customers.

The past may provide some insight into your personality

Volumes have been written on how parents affect the makeup of our personality. While psychoanalysis is not in the scope of this book, it is useful to consider how upbringing may affect your behavior and success in life.

Often there exists a competition for energy between individuals that usually displays itself as interrupting others in a conversation and other subtle discourtesies. You need to look deeper at personalities to understand why people react the way they do. You can bring counterproductive behavior into dealings with people without even being aware of it. If you hope to establish solid relationships with your customers, you must go beyond the surface level of communication that consists of small talk followed by a sales dialog.

Many of the conflicts and misunderstandings between people occur because of a competition for energy. Certainly people rise to higher positions in companies because of a desire for power, inflated egos, or any other number of reasons. It is helpful to recognize the positions customers hold; often it may reveal their motives, deeply help values, and reasons for buying. Positions of authority attract people who enjoy being in charge of other people.

People act out "programmed responses" that are more or less created by family interactions. While all people combine different aspects, one usually dominates the scene. Parents that intimidate or interrogate, can produce a tendency in their children to withdraw and feel sorry for themselves. A parent who yells and intimidates creates fear; the natural response is that of helplessness. An interrogator parent creates the response of aloofness since, after all, why answer a question if you are berated for it. On the flip side, parents who have taken on the helplessness theme can instill the qualities of intimidation in their children. Parents who tend to be vague and aloof more or less create an inquisitive, or interrogator child.

If you think back to events in your childhood, it should be clear how your parents treated you and how you responded to this treatment. Think about it now. Was your father an intimidator and mother an interrogator? Vice versa? Or did one or both tend towards self pity or aloofness? Whatever the situation, if you know what your reaction is when relating to different behavior, you can stop it and move toward accomplishing your interpersonal communication objective.

Make some notes below concerning your parents personalities. How did you respond the their particular programmed response? Do you react to people today with the same programmed response as you did with your parents? Recognizing a situation is the first step in changing it to a more favorable and desirable outcome. With some deliberate effort we all have the ability to overcome our childhood programming.

_____

_____

_____

_____

_____

_____

_____

_____

_____

_____

_____

_____

_____

_____

_____

_____

_____

_____

_____

_____

_____

_____

_____

Chapter Ten

The Power of the Purpose Statement

Make certain you like the way you present yourself

Before discussing purpose statements, it is important to look at what precedes this in a sales call; the way in which you present yourself. This has a significant impact on your success in selling. Your image and the way you present yourself includes more than outward appearance alone.

While your physical appearance is important, it is only part of the picture. What the customer sees is, in part, what you have created in you own mind. Self-image ultimately determines outward appearance. Do you like the way you look? If so, great. If not, you must do something to change your perception of your appearance.

It may be as simple as allowing yourself to buy more nice suits or jackets, or attending a seminar on image enhancement and self-improvement. Knowing the importance of your self-image and that it requires attention is the first step toward improvement. If there are things you cannot change physically, you can certainly consult an image specialist or even sales clerks from some of the better clothing stores. They will go to great lengths to help you look your best. And remember, you do not have to look like a model to be respected.

A lack of confidence sends people the wrong signal that you may have something to hide. This is the last thing you need in the profession of selling, where it is tough enough to get attention. A neatly-dressed person with an honest friendly attitude is more approachable than an exceptionally good-looking person without this trait.

Clothing can help flatter physical appearance, but if you have a self-esteem problem with some physical attribute, recognize this and take steps to remedy it. Most people do not look like fashion models, and success is guaranteed more by confidence than looks.

Below, list all the things you like about yourself and those that need improvement. Include mental and physical aspects of appearance in your list. This will be revealing, especially if you are honest and allow yourself to get the most out of this exercise. Make the list right now.

My Assets (don't be modest!)	Things I Need To Improve

Look for the good in all people and situations

In addition to the physical side, you must consider that what you are feeling shows in your body posture and facial expressions. If you happen to be having a bad day, your negative emotions will show. Do not deny the fact that you are in a bad mood, but make the best of a less-than-desirable situation. Occasionally you may have to force a smile. In addition to this, work hard at looking for the *good* in people and events that happen during your day.

Take some time now to plan some action steps to improve your self-image. Again, it may be as simple as shopping for some new business attire, or beginning a new diet and fitness program. Whether it is one event or a series of steps, schedule it in your daily calendar now.

Have a strong, one sentence, purpose statement for every sales call

The way you look and carry yourself influences how well you are received by your customers. When you see a customer for the first time you can bet they are wondering, "Who is this person and why are they here? Is this person just going to push me into buying something like most sales people do?" These are some of the questions your prospects are thinking when you come calling.

The first words out of your mouth are scrutinized very closely. Unless you have a strong purpose statement that gets the prospect's attention and creates interest, you are on your way out the door. When you use the telephone to set up an appointment, the need for a good strong purpose statement is greater. It is easier to say no to someone over the telephone than in person.

Often sales people get the big brush off because the purpose statement is not intriguing enough to warrant further listening. Sometimes customers are actually too busy to see you. But if they will not take the time to schedule a future appointment, you can be sure you have not created enough interest.

Most customers have a "hot button" or something that gets them motivated. If you cannot create enough interest with your superior market offer, perhaps other things will interest a customer. Offering to take a difficult-to-see customer to lunch, on the sole premise of getting to understand their business needs better, is an excellent strategy. Some customers want free tickets to a ball game and will outright tell you that "greasing their palms" is the only way to do business with them. Be careful in these situations; rarely is the cost worth the benefit. Customers like this are loyal to whoever happens to be giving them the nicest perks, so use it as a last resort. Bringing in food, dessert, or other perks is much like a personal gift; it is more appreciated when the motive is sincere and the receiver is not expecting it.

Prepare for every sales call

Planning and goal setting were covered in Chapter Six. Planning and preparation determine your ability to customize and deliver an effective purpose statement. Knowing an account history or potential before you walk in the door gives you an advantage. You are more likely to be taken seriously when you have information specific to that customer incorporated into your dialog. "Hi, I'm Bob with XYZ company. I talked to Becky last week about saving her some money on her production costs. Would it be possible for me to meet with her this morning or would this afternoon be better?" This is specific, to the point, and demonstrates that Becky will probably want to see you.

Utilize all company reports that provide you with customer information and spend the time to review them before every sales call. This only takes a few minutes and can greatly increase your chances to see the decision maker. It also enhances your credibility and shows that you are there for a specific purpose and not just a routine visit. As a professional salesperson you want to be taken seriously and respected by your customers— preparation and planning will help you gain this respect.

Gather information on each and every sales call

On every sales call, your goal should be to make some kind of impact. If you create interest, project a good image, and gather useful information, the sales call is successful. Even if you do not sell anything, your time has been well spent. In fact it is probably best *not* to try to sell something the first time you meet a prospect. Why? Their guard is up and they are usually prepared to say "no", regardless of your proposal. You may even want to *promise* not to attempt to sell them anything. The suspense can build their interest and they may realize that you have a strong story to tell about your product.

Remember, people want what they cannot have. Have a strong reason why your prospect should listen to what you have to say, even if it is only to meet you. This alone can be used as a reason to see a customer. "I have never met Ms. Williams, and wanted to take one minute or less to introduce myself," can be an effective purpose statement especially when calling on new customers who are difficult to see.

Purpose statements on future calls have to be more creative. A good strategy here is to always leave the call with something you need to follow up on. This can be an idea, a product sample, or something else that requires followup. Before saying good-bye you might say something like, "I'll check back with you in three weeks to get your opinion on ABC. Is that OK?" Mentioning this to the receptionist virtually sets up your next appointment.

Sell everyone involved in the outcome of the sale, on the importance of your purpose

Many times you will not be talking to the decision maker initially. Whoever you talk to needs to be sold on why they should let you see the decision maker. These "gatekeepers," or "guard dogs" as they are often referred to, are your first sale. They must be convinced that what you will offer their supervisor or colleague is of value. They are an individual just as the decision maker is. Be empathic of their situation by showing some genuine concern for their position and status in the organization. This is something most salespeople do not do. Besides, it will make you feel more benevolent and brighten up their day as well. The small courtesies we share or bestow on people have more impact and are appreciated more than the so-called "big favors."

Why is it so important to sell the reception person on your importance? Put yourself in their shoes. Their reputation is on the line. Convince them to let you see the prospect, and come through with a useful proposal, and you make *them* look good in their supervisor's eye. Having a strong purpose statement shows you are an important person who values time. Wasting their supervisor's time has the opposite effect.

Another thing to always keep in mind: *your time* and your *prospect's time*. Respect them both. You will stand out from the crowd of salespeople who say, "I just want to take two minutes of your time," and then lecture for fifteen. (They do one thing they said they were going to do, *take* the prospects time.) Always say what you are going to do, and then stick by it, no matter what. "I would like to introduce myself to Mr./Ms. Smith and give a brief three-minute synopsis of our business services. In this much time we will both know if I can save your organization money by reducing your costs." This statement is concise, non-threatening, and mentions the possible benefit. Again, you may want to even promise *not* to try to sell them anything today. This shows two things: one, you are a person of your word (integrity) and two, you are probably someone you will be around after the sale. Since you are taking the time to truly learn about possible problems *before* you offer solutions, you are gaining respect in their eyes. Remember, one of the goals of reception staff is to make sure their supervisors time is not wasted. You must show them in a few seconds that you have something of value to share.

Avoid offering premature solutions

Most salespeople propose a product or service as a solution before they uncover the prospect's needs. How would you like to go to the doctor who looks at you for one minute and pre-scribes treatment or medication? You would never listen to their diagnosis again, right? It's the same with a typical "feature/benefit" sales presentation. Don't do it! You blow your cred-ibility right off the bat and lose any chance of doing business with this person.

You will learn how to ask the right questions in the next chapter, but remember to ask questions before you discuss the details of a product or service. Remember that part of your customer's fear in making a purchase involves you and your company. They are asking themselves if you and the company have the ability to follow through with what you say you and your product or service will do.

Do not project solutions based on how you do it

Many people project a standard prescription as a solution to other people's problems. This prescription is based on their own interpretation and perspective.

Only when you first understand the other person's viewpoint can you begin to recommend an appropriate course of action. Empathy and understanding different personality styles is necessary.

Chapter Eleven

The Power of Questions

Your goal is to establish a long-term relationship

The previous chapter on the purpose statement is only the beginning of a successful and personalized sales call. During the entire presentation, keep in mind that you are attempting to establish a long-term relationship. Regardless of the type of business you are in, new customers are difficult to find.

You want to establish long-term repeat sales with satisfied customers. With this worthy goal constantly in mind, you will avoid saying and doing things that prevent good customer relations. This is the only way to do business in today's competitive environment. Before getting into the power of questions, lets look at some preliminary steps.

Once you have stated your purpose and gained attention, be courteous and immediately thank the customer for giving you some time. Confirm how much time they have to spend with you and honor it to the last second. If they say "I only have a minute," honor it literally. You can accomplish a lot in this minute—find out their business needs, establish a future date when they have more time, and demonstrate that you are person of your word and finish in one minute. Honest, you will stand out from the crowd of "My Product" sales people who go on babbling for ten minutes about how great their product is. Do not give your customer a valid reason to never see you again.

Most of the time the customer will ask more questions after you point out that your time is up. They are giving you license to talk more, but be careful not to abuse it. When you are given only a minute or so, don't try to close the sale. Unless you are further along in the sales process, closing so quickly is sloppy and unprofessional. A quick close may also result in obtaining a smaller order than you would have obtained with a thorough sales call. Make an appointment in the near future so you can spend time establishing a relationship that leads to quality long term, repeat sales.

A good sales call sounds like a conversation

Ask questions in such a way that the prospect *knows* you care about their business problems. Many books and training courses on selling reveal their true foundation when they say something like, "Ask questions that make the prospect think you care about him or her." If you do not truly care about your customers, you should be selling another product or service and chances are you will be, sooner or later.

Be conversational and avoid the trap of turning into an interrogator and playing verbal ping-pong. Ask a few key open-ended questions that encourage the customer to talk and give you information. Open-ended questions cannot be answered with a simple yes or no. They usually begin with, "Tell me about your....." or the classic, who, what, why, where, when.

Avoid the temptation to interrupt and interject ideas during the time the customer is opening up to you. Let them complete all their thoughts. Truly listen. Take notes to prevent forgetting key points and some important purpose your product or service can fill for the customer. This type of genuine listening demonstrates that you care about the customer.

Use good eye contact and make sure your body language shows that you are listening and interested in the customer. Folding your arms across your chest sends the wrong message and is a distraction to the customer. Be conscious of your distance as every individual has a different idea of how close you can get before you are "in their face." Standing beside a customer is a good way to get close. Standing face-to-face can sometimes appear confrontational and works against your objective.

Who, what, where, why, and when, are open-ended questions that need to be asked and answered. The five W's, as they are called, are good to remember in order to monitor your progress in uncovering your customers needs. If you truly become concerned with your prospect's needs you will be more tactful when asking these open-ended questions. They can be used in a conversational manner such as this: "Mr. Jones, now that you know who I am and what our company does, do you mind if I ask you a few questions in order to see if we can assist your business? What product do you currently use? Why do use that product/service? Where and how often do you purchase it?" Try to integrate *conversation* relating to the customer's answers after each question. This keeps the sales call more personal and avoids the feeling of an interrogation. This is a great technique for uncovering a customer's mindset on the way they do business. The answers reveal much about a customer's philosophy and help you get an understanding of how you can tailor your product or service to meet their special needs.

Close-ended questions are used when you desire specific information. They require a simple yes, no, or a short answer and are useful once open-ended questions have uncovered key information. There is a danger in using close-ended questions, or closed probes, since they can have the effect of ending a sales call early. Asking a customer, "Do you use this type product?" could be answered with a resounding "no." It is difficult to pick up the momentum of a sales call after such a response. Many salespeople use closed probes only when they can be answered with a "yes." These probes are sometimes referred to as "tie-downs" and consist of a series of closed probes that will guarantee a yes response. The philosophy is that the more times a customer says yes, the more likely you are to get a yes when you ask for the order.

There is a danger you should be aware of in selling based solely on the customer's feedback. In an effort to make your product or service fit their current system, you may miss an opportunity to introduce a new and different, perhaps better, system to the customer. A tactful way to introduce a new concept is to ask, "Mr. Jones, your system has worked great for you and I can see why you might not see a need to change. I have a new idea and if you would not mind, I would like to ask your opinion. How about...." State the new concept and perhaps let the customer introduce their own ideas. Think of it as a brainstorming session with your customer. If they feel that the idea is theirs, and buy it, they will be a loyal customer.

Qualify, Quantify, and search for Hotbuttons

Well before your close, as covered in the next chapter, you must qualify and quantify your customer's potential need for your product. Ask some questions to find out what they need. Two good questions that accomplish this are: "What do you like about your current product?" and "What one or two things would you improve if you could?" Ask the questions in this order to prevent the customer from reselling themselves on their current product. Do let them carry on too long about how great their current product and supplier is. Ask how much they currently use and how often they need to order. This gives you information that will help you close the sale later on.

It is very likely the customer will reveal their *hotbutton*—their main reason for buying. "You know I would really like a product..." is a reply that gives you the information you need to target your presentation around their hotbutton.

Negative selling is unprofessional and counterproductive

Never negative-sell. Sell your product or service on its merits alone. Every product has strong points. Learn what yours are and capitalize on them. If you must mention a competitor, never use the brand or company name. Say "other companies" and keep references very general. You don't want to give your competitor free advertising.

Sometimes your customers will set you up and encourage you to negative-sell so they can brush you off. Do not fall for it. Negative selling reinforces the idea that you do not have a good product offer that can stand on its own merits. Concede that the product they are using is a good product, but that there may be some advantages to using yours. In a consultant role, tell them you simply want to be sure that they have all the information so that they can make the wisest decision.

Telling a prospect or customer that the product they are

using is inferior or overpriced is the equivalent of calling them stupid. It's like saying, "Hey, you made a really stupid choice buying that, but listen to me, I have something better." It goes over like a lead balloon; they hear the first few words out of your mouth and then tune you out.

In a situation where a competitive company is spreading blatant untruths about your product, take a pro-active approach. You might say, "Some of our competitors are stating that...I wanted to take this opportunity to give you the latest information so you can make the best decision. Don't take my word for it here is the proof..." Again, never mention the product or company. You can be sure that the customer will take note when the competitive rep comes around next time.

The point is, who is more credible in the customers eyes? Your purpose is not to ruin the credibility of the other representative, rather to take the opportunity to prove that you are a resource the customer can count on. The other representative ruined credibility by stating information that was unsubstantiated. You want your actions to demonstrate that you are the more mature professional.

Sell your product or service based on what it can do for the customer

Always sell your product on its merits. This is done, obviously, only after you have established rapport and gathered enough information about the customer's needs. This is the most effective way to combat a competitor's product. Use the words feel, felt, and found to deal with objections. "We use XYZ and have for years. It works well and I cannot imagine switching." A good response that avoids negative selling would be, "XYZ is a fine product; I understand how you **feel**. I have had many customers who **felt** that way before they saw the benefits of PQR. Once they did, they **found** that PQR gave them even *better* results than they were previously getting."

Of course this approach only works if you really do have a competitive advantage. It is worth repeating that it is your responsibility to your *company*, your *customer*, and *yourself* to learn every possible advantage your product has over the competition. See Chapter Three, "Knowing Your Stuff."

Some products have one or two big features that are key considerations the customer uses to make a purchase decision. Other products have many smaller factors that when combined convince the customer to purchase. The decision to purchase a new home is a good example. The size of home, the neighborhood, and other big features narrow down the field of possible choices. Among those homes that qualify the one that *feels* the best is usually the one with several desirable smaller features— trees in the backyard, new windows, new appliances, new carpets, and the like.

Never refer to your product or service as "our"

It may seem a small point, but it is very significant in the business of selling. The importance of the customer taking ownership of what you are offering is critical to the close of a sale and long-term satisfaction. They have to feel that it is truly their product. Instead of saying, "Our product will make your clients...," use the brand name of your product. "XYZ will make your clients..." Even better is to refer to it as "theirs." "Your new system will maximize your ability..." This is a very subtle but powerful point you should keep in mind during your presentations.

Do not play verbal ping-pong with your customers

Needs-based selling has been taught under several names: professional selling skills, needs satisfaction selling, but the system is the same in all programs. Many companies purchased the training modules from the Xerox Corporation.

There is a sequence in this selling system that goes as follows: **Probe** to uncover the prospects needs; **Support** those needs with a support statement; **Close** by summarizing the benefits accepted and request a commitment. The model describes techniques for handling prospect attitudes of skepticism, indifference and objection. The needs-based selling system is good but is overly simplistic and often makes the customer feel "set up."

A typical dialog would be: (Salesrep Open-probe), "Mr. Smith, tell me about some of your current equipment demands." (Reply), "We utilize all our machines to their maximum and get adequate results with the brand we currently use." (Salesrep reply), "Could your business benefit from a faster system than the one you currently have?" (Reply), "Yes, we could benefit from a faster system." (Sales Support Statement), "You are right, most businesses such as yours increase productivity and hence profits when they switch to a faster system. XYZ brand has been proven to..." (At this stage, if the customer gives buying signals—head nodding yes, "Sounds Good," or any other positive statements—the close is attempted). If the customer exhibits skepticism, indifference or objections, the system calls for more questions followed by the above sequence of supporting and closing.

When a salesperson relies exclusively on one of the needs-based selling systems, empathy and listening skills are thrown aside. The salesperson is so caught up in the system thinking about what step is next, they forget to listen and really hear what the customer is trying to tell them. The system can force the salesperson to cram customers into categories, such as skeptical, indifferent, or objectionable.

The methods for handling such customers become perfunctory at best and confrontational in the worst situations. Customers feel as though they are being "set up" and that a verbal ping-pong match is underway. They may even say, "You guys ask too many questions, just tell me what you have." Now here is a logical personality telling you their needs.

According to the needs-based selling system, there is no reply for this other than starting over with the same question game originally implemented. Respect the customer's wishes, explain what you have and, in subtle ways, find out what some of the business needs are.

You may need to rely on the customer's associates for much of the information. Attempt a subtle close only if it feels appropriate. Avoid pushing for the sale on that first call as most sales training systems recommend. Followup later and ask for the order. Make sure you do not use selling techniques in place of intuition and common sense. Customers want and deserve to be treated as individuals; nothing turns them off more than a canned presentation for the masses.

Get the customer involved!

Asking questions is only part of the presentation process. It is worth mentioning some important aspects of presentation skills. Once you have uncovered some key needs or wants that your customer has, use this information to customize your presentation. If you sell a product that has a taste or feel or smell, you are lucky. Getting a customer involved using as many senses as possible helps them take ownership of the product. Humans are by nature very sensory-oriented. Use this to create involvement on the part of your customer.

If you sell a service, involving the senses in your presentation is more of a challenge but it can be done. Even if you sell financial products or insurance you can get the customer involved through writing. Suggest that they might want to take notes or write down some figures you are quoting. It is better to have them write down information than to have you do it for them. *Involvement* of any type will move you closer to creating a sale.

Utilize visual aids during all your presentations. Be careful not to introduce them too early in the presentation, making sure you have created interest and qualified the customer first. Visual aids usually contain many words so be sure to point out only those words that help you make your point—do not allow the customer to read the entire brochure. A customer's questions are good but not if they ruin the flow of your presentation and cause confusion. Maintain possession of visual aids as this prevents you from losing control of the presentation and becoming sidetracked. The same rules apply to samples of product.

Structure your sales presentation so that it begins with general product information and progresses to specific product information. Involve the customer in every step by asking for feedback periodically. "What do you think so far?" is a good question that keeps the customer from getting lost during the presentation and also creates involvement along the way.

Good questions can make negative situations work for you

Well-asked questions can be used in other situations besides the actual sale. As a sales person, do not forget the importance of service after the sale. Taking the time to followup after a sale is a great way to prevent small issues from becoming major problems. It also goes a long way to demonstrate that you are an unusual salesperson who really cares. Questions can be used to turn an apparent negative situation into an opportunity to become a resource to your customers.

A phone call from an angry customer who receives an incorrect or defective product, is a common situation all sales people deal with. Rather than assuming they want to return the product, respond with a heartfelt apology. In the customer's eyes your company has caused grief. No matter whose fault it was, you have to make the customer happy or lose them as a customer forever. Passing on blame in these situations does nothing but put gasoline on the fire. After receiving a response to the apology, ask, "What can I do to make this situation right and keep you as a customer?" You will find that in most cases the customer will change moods from combative to cordial. They may discover they can use the product anyway, but just felt that they had to speak their mind and let someone know that a mistake was made. Most customers are not so forthright in their true motives, but this is a good example of how simple it can be to fix what appears to be a big problem. Good questions and listening are all that it takes.

Seminar presentations reinforce your consultant status

In the beginning of this book it was pointed out that the goal was not to give you 101 different selling tips. Sales presentations must be personalized, based on the company and the product or service sold. The goal of this book is to provide a foundation for you to learn what you need to do to succeed and enjoy your profession.

Seminar selling is one type of presentation that can help accomplish this goal regardless of what industry you sell in. Financial, pharmaceutical, computer—just about any product offered—can be presented in a seminar forum. How you organize these seminars depends on your customers and where they are found. The place may vary from a small lunchroom to a convention hall.

The impact on your success as a salesperson can be astronomical. Your ability to emphasize the strong points of your product or service is enhanced because you have a captive audience and the time to spend with them. You establish rapport, long-term relationships and even friendships. Often you learn more about competitive products and industry trends, especially if you allow time in your presentation for questions and comments. You feel more professional and effective than a "regular" sales call, since your time is spent more efficiently. Seminars are a great tool to sell more and enjoy your job more.

The next, and last, chapter brings together all of the concepts in this book. Closing the sale is the ultimate goal of every sales call.

Chapter Twelve

Customizing the Close

Most sales training manuals and books are full of techniques for closing the sale. Unfortunately many of these techniques do little to encourage an amiable long-term relationship with the customer. They hint at arm-twisting and trickery in order to get the prospect to buy today. Do not use any techniques for closing a sale that talks down to or patronizes your customers. Winning one sale is not worth sacrificing years of potential business.

The "puppy dog" close and the "Ben Franklin" close can yield sales. If your customers resent buying, they will not become long-term customers. Why? Because they will resent you for pushing them.

The "puppy dog" close, referenced in many selling books, refers to any technique that lets the customer try the product or service. The idea is that once the customer "takes it home" they will fall in love with it and decide to keep it.

The Ben Franklin close refers to the technique suggested by Benjamin Franklin when trying to make a decision. On one side of the paper the positive aspects are listed and on the other, the negative. The salesperson lists the positive aspects of the product or service, and then hands the paper to the prospect and asks them to list the negative aspects. The theory is that the positives aspects of the product or service will outnumber the negatives and the customer will be compelled to buy. Many people would be put off and feel manipulated by this approach. Even if you could get them to play along and fill out their half of the list, they still would not buy unless *they* were ready.

The closing technique is not as important as the work that should *precede* the close of a sale. All the material in this book is meant to help you develop the understanding and qualities required before a close.

Take an extreme example. How successful would you be selling your product or service if you walked in the door for the first time and the first words out of your mouth were, "Will you buy this from me?" Not very good, right? Many sales people are guilty of doing just this when they rely on closing techniques instead of hard preliminary selling skills.

It is ideal to uncover needs first, but customers often do not know they want your product until they see it. Presenting a product and asking for feedback along the way is a great way to *build* need. As mentioned in the previous chapter, ask for feedback during your presentation. "What do you think?" and "Does this make sense?" are two good questions that give you the feedback you need and also serve as small *trial closes*. This feedback helps keep your presentation on track and assures that you are connecting with the customer. If a customer agrees during a presentation that a proposal "sounds good" he or she is likely to buy when the final close is attempted. Avoid a long lecture that does not allow the customer the opportunity to ask questions.

Always sell in such a way that the customer feels good about the purchase

Remind customers of your product guarantees or personal assurances of followup and service—whatever it takes to make them feel good about their purchase. Never sell unless they customer *buys*. Closing a sale should feel natural when you have done your homework, studied your product and your customer. The sale follows naturally.

Professional salespeople do not really sell; they help prospects make informed decisions to *buy* from them. This subtle difference is very significant. When a customer says, "You know, I think it would benefit us to start using this product," they have committed to their decision and a solid sale is made. When you reach this level of selling you will have customers who are loyal to you for years. This type of customer returns less product than other customers, and becomes your best form of advertising through referrals.

Sales can be closed using more manipulative techniques, but they are flimsy sales that result in returns, or worse, an unhappy customer.

Make a conscious effort to close once the ground work has been done

Closing techniques *are* important and you do need to make a conscious effort to close the sale after you have done all the hard preliminary work. Most sales are made after several closing attempts. There are many types of salespeople but there are few good closers.

Some salespeople are simply order-takers and use small talk and personal charm combined with luck to stay in the game.

They do nothing to generate new business or understand their customers needs. They are diligent in *visiting* their customers and this alone keeps them in the average performance category. It is true that simply contacting your customers regularly can guarantee a significant amount of business. But sales people who make a constant, conscientious effort to close the sale are at the top with regard to performance and career fulfillment. After all your preliminary sales work, you owe it to yourself, your company, and your customer to ask for the order. The previous chapter pointed out the importance of qualifying and quantifying customers as well finding hotbuttons.

Make it a point to find at least one good personal quality in every customer

What does it take to close successfully and in such a way that your customer still says "thank you" after you write up the order? First, you must *like* your customer; they must like you; they must listen and believe what you have to say. This simplifies the process described earlier, but this sequence must happen to create solid long-term satisfied customers.

Think about it. Have you ever liked someone without them liking you? For a short while perhaps, but not for long. You do not have to like everything about a person, but you must find something about them—family, hobbies, community service—that you do like, and compliment them on it. When it is done sincerely it creates good will. Your customer already knows this is a good trait. By pointing it out, you have shown a personal interest. It can be tough with some customers who seem to be downright nasty people, and it may take you a while to come up with something. But if you hope to sell to a wide variety of personalities, you must believe there is something good inside of every individual.

For hesitant customers, minimize the pain of the decision with a "small" trial order

Good closers know the strong points of their products and how to emphasize them in a positive light. They are creative, finding original solutions to potential problems before they get blown out of proportion. They are helpful and go the extra mile doing whatever it takes to satisfy the customers, within reason.

They ask for the order. This sounds obvious, but many salespeople do not ask. Why not just present your material and let the customer tell you if they want to order?

We are all driven by a fear of failure or a desire for gain when faced with a decision. If the desire for gain outweighs the fear, the customer leaps at the opportunity to buy. You have heard the expression, "I don't have anything to lose."Obviously, the risk of making a poor decision is minimal when a person proclaims this.

Usually the customer's primary hang-up with buying is fear of making the wrong decision. This is the failure. Your job as a good closer is to minimize the pain involved in purchasing. Remind the customer of the benefits of your product or service. Emphasize the money-back guarantee, small minimum order, anything and everything to simplify the buying process.

A good simple close might be something like this, "You can try a case of 12, or you could start out with a *small* case of just six units." This works well with overly-cautious customers. If you have done your preliminary sales work, the customer should say yes. You take them off the hook from making a "big commitment" to a new product by suggesting they *try* a "small order."

Reducing to the ridiculous is another way to get the customer over their fear of making a huge financial or long-term mistake. When you look at the cost-per-day, per unit, per application, you can usually demonstrate that a product or service can be very economical. Life insurance companies use this technique constantly, "Only $1.25 per day". If you use this technique, make sure it does not sound phony, and that the savings is significant for the customer.

Use silence after your close

Be completely silent after your close, and do not say a word until the customer responds. Once you've asked for the order, the customer must say yes or no. Let them respond. "Would you like to give it a try?" followed by silence, is one of the most effective closes available, provided all the preliminary sales work has been done. It's a pity to lose a sale after all the hard work has been done and the customer is ready to buy. Many salespeople blow a deal and let the customer off the hook because they do not know how to sit back and be quiet.

Your last chance

For customers that; show interest in your product, answer "yes" to your trial closes, but still do not want to buy, try the following. Once your product has been presented and your offer rejected begin to gather up your materials. Thank the customer for their time and then ask if there is any other issue that may be preventing them from trying your product. "What would it take for you to consider using XYZ?" is a good question that may uncover the customer's true objection. Many customers are simply afraid of making a buying decision and the fact that they think the sales call is over puts them at ease—a relaxed customer is more likely to buy. This is usually the case with defensive customers.

There may be a simple issue that you can remedy to help move the sale forward. Even if this strategy does not yield a sale immediately the information obtained makes a future sale more likely.

Close for a commitment for those "I'll think it over customers"

One of the biggest frustrations in sales is the "I'll think it over and get back to you" brush off. Many salespeople new to the profession actually expect the customer to call back. Usually this is a hollow promise and the customer is hiding the real objection. Other times the customer means to get back to you but simply forgets. Either way the end result is that you do not hear back from them and nothing gets sold.

When you get this response to a close attempt, reply, "Great, I'm happy that you will give our ...your consideration. Is there any other information that I can get you that will assist in your decision?" (This may get them to reveal the real objection if there is one.) After a reply from the customer, qualify when and who will help decide, and schedule a specific time that you will check back. Even if they give you no specific time ask, "Can I followup and check back with you in one week, or would two weeks be better?" "Who should I talk to when I call?" Continue this even if, on your followup, you get the same reply. An order or a definite "no" with a specific reason why, should be your only reason for not continuing to followup. If you do get a definite "no," be understanding and ask a few more questions to make sure you have a clear picture of the reasons why they have decided against your offer.

Look at every objection as a question

When a customer raises an objection to your product or company, reword it as a question. "I do not want to switch to your product now" should be reworded to: "Why should I switch to your product? Show me the reasons."

Handle price objections skillfully

Price is almost always an issue for the customer. Some customers are hung up on this more than others. There are those customers that always buy the cheapest product, but most understand the concept of good value and the idea that "you get what you pay for."

If you sell the low-cost version of a popular product your job is easy when it comes to handling the price conscious customer—you simply state the price. If you sell a premium product then you must get the chance for the customer to hear your complete story before you disclose the price. "How much does it cost," are often the first words to come out of some customer's mouths. A good way to put this off until later without sounding evasive is to reply, "PQR costs between $25 and $65, depending on your typical order. How many units do you order per year?" Use specific numbers only if you are competitive, otherwise say, "It depends on the quantity." This gives you the opportunity to qualify your customer, but make sure you quickly get off the topic of price. Ask the customer, "Is it OK if I quickly show your some of the features of this product before we discuss price?"

Get the customer excited and interested in the product and then show how the price is justified. This depends on the nature of your individual product. Show how the product saves money over time or reduces maintenance costs, etc.

Use testimonials and proof sources

Hesitant customers that give you the "I'll think it over" routine usually have some other reason for deciding not to purchase your product. Often they are not convinced that your product will do what you say it will do, or that you or your company will do what you say you will do.

Make it a habit to collect testimonial letters from your most satisfied customers. Try to get a variety—some that praise you, your company, and your product. Having these letters can often help close a sale with a skeptical or indifferent customer. Offer to show them to the customer at appropriate times during your presentation or as a last attempt to create interest.

Keep copies of any good reviews your company receives in papers and magazines. If you sell a technical product maintain a good supply of relevant support literature.

Followup after the sale to increase product or service usage

Make sure you followup and give good customer service to insure that the customer increases usage, and commits completely to your product. Once a sale is made, do not drop the ball and forget to coach your customers. Some need more coaching than others, but all customers need to be reminded regularly why they bought your product or service and how to best utilize it. Some products and services are very technical and obviously require this "coaching." Other products may be simple, but the customer may need some extra help because they are new in their business.

New business is important, but repeat business is a major

goal of any company. You can increase this through good service and followup. Depending on the nature of your product you want to expand current usage to other areas, if at all possible. The cellular phone industry has been doing a great job increasing usage of their products and services by stressing the importance of having a phone in your car in case of an emergency. Companies that sell services usually have a better chance expanding usage than those that sell products, but there are exceptions. Markets for food products can be expanded by including recipes for desserts and other dishes on the package. Be creative and do not be afraid to suggest ideas that appear obvious; the marketing department cannot always think of everything.

Personal notes have a long-term impact

Taking the time to write a personal note of thank you to a customer, and even a colleague, goes a long way to create a long-term relationship. Notes also make the job of selling more personal, and this results in feeling good about your profession, your job, and yourself. People tend to read personally written notes more often than form letters or standard print on a brochure.

Obviously, a great time to write a note to a customer is after the sale. Any occasion that warrants followup is appropriate as well. Use this tool to improve your selling results and personalize your selling style. Ask the customer for referrals of people they know that might be interested in your offering.

It is appropriate to mention that you should never discuss politics, religion or other emotionally charged issues while making small-talk with your customers. If you are asked directly what your view is on a sensitive issue, concede that it is complicated and that there is no clear answer.

Be creative

Good salespeople use creative solutions to solve problems. As mentioned before, selling is a type of negotiation. Win-win negotiations, where both parties are satisfied, is the goal when you establish a long-term business relationship with a customer.

When customers articulate that they are unhappy with an outcome, do your best to remedy the situation as soon as possible. Ask the customers what they want. Often it is something simple to fulfill. Many customers simply want to blow off steam; all they want is someone to listen with empathy. Sometimes a free sample or other simple gesture goes a long way to patch up a sticky situation.

Avoid confrontation when dealing with customer complaints. It is easy to react to a customer's accusations, but do your best to remain detached from the situation. The problem has already occurred; your job now is to solve the problem to the customer's satisfaction. Many salespeople are more concerned with saving face and not being blamed for the problem than they are with finding a solution. Apologize sincerely and find a solution as soon as possible.

Perhaps a customer was mistreated by someone in your company in the past. There is nothing you can do about this, but you can work hard to show them that you are different. Remember, actions speak louder than words, and customers that have been mistreated in the past will be watching all you do.

Conclusion

In summary, remember to always put your customer's needs first. Sell what is right for them in the long run and you will be rewarded. Be a constant student of business and industry learning and keep your mind open to changes within your company and industry. When you work in an industry that fits your personality, you have a real foundation for success. Enthusiasm and product knowledge come that much easier when you feel comfortable with your work. Expect a sale every time you are talking to a qualified customer, because this expectation can become a reality in your success.

This book should deliver on its promise to you. Use it as a reference source as you progress in your sales career. There is ample room at the end of this chapter for notes. Use it as you see fit, writing personal ideas on selling, your company, and your industry. Your ideas, combined with the concepts in this book, will help you gain a better understanding into your profession. You will be confident about where you fit in and how you can better yourself and your career.

This pro-active approach will contribute to satisfaction and enjoyment. You will know in what direction you need to move to make things better. Action in any direction is what we all need to get out of ruts, personal or professional. When you have a personal action plan, getting stuck is less likely. Understanding a situation is the first step. Then decide on an action plan, and act on that plan.

Utilize your daily planner as your primary organizational tool. It is the key to better action plans. Remember to treat yourself better than you would any other irreplaceable asset.

May you find success and enjoyment in selling.

NOTES

NOTES

Index

We would like to hear from you!

We would like your feedback. Feel free to let us know how this book has helped you. Please use specific stories on how the concepts in this book have been applied and resulted in a success. If the information in this book has contributed to job satisfaction or selling success let us know.

Also, if you have ideas that enhance concepts in this book let us know. These ideas may be included in future editions of Successful Enjoyable Selling and you will be recognized in the acknowledgment section. You can write or call:

Rainier Publishing
P.O. Box 46491
Seattle, WA 98146
(206) 932-8416

Also you can e-mail the author at pwrichards@msn.com

Order Form

Please send the following books:
I understand that I may return any books for a
full refund—for any reason, no questions asked.

Successful Enjoyable Selling $9.95 Quantity_____

Company name:_____

Name:_____

Address:_____

City:_____State:_____Zip:_____

Sales tax:
Please add 8% to $9.95 for books shipped to Washington
addresses

Shipping:
Book Rate: $2.00 for the first book and 75 cents for each
additional book (Surface shipping may take three to four
weeks) Air mail: $3.50 per book.

Mail check or money order to:

Rainier Publishing
P.O. Box 46491
Seattle, WA 98146

Order Form

Please send the following books:

_____ and _____ that I may return any book for a full refund, for any reason, no questions asked.

_____ Superior Cribbage, price: $9.95 each _____

Company name _____

Name _____

Address _____

City _____ State _____ Zip _____

Sales Tax:
Please add 8% sales tax for books shipped to Washington addresses.

Shipping:
Book Rate: $2.00 for the first book and 75¢ for each additional book. Shipping may take three to four weeks. Air Mail: $3.50 per book.

Send check or money order to:

Eldora Publishing
PO Box 46201
Seattle, WA 98146

Order Form

Please send the following books:
I understand that I may return any books for a
full refund—for any reason, no questions asked.

Successful Enjoyable Selling $9.95 Quantity_____

Company name:_____

Name:_____

Address:_____

City:_____State:_____Zip:_____

Sales tax:
Please add 8% to $9.95 for books shipped to Washington
 addresses

Shipping:
Book Rate: $2.00 for the first book and 75 cents for each
additional book (Surface shipping may take three to four
weeks) Air mail: $3.50 per book.

Mail check or money order to:

Rainier Publishing
P.O. Box 46491
Seattle, WA 98146